A CONCISE HISTORY
OF AMERICAN MUSIC
EDUCATION

MICHAEL L. MARK

Published in partnership with
MENC: The National Association for Music Education
Frances S. Ponick, Executive Editor

ROWMAN & LITTLEFIELD EDUCATION
Lanham • New York • Toronto • Plymouth, UK

Published in partnership with
MENC: The National Association for Music Education

Published in the United States of America
by Rowman & Littlefield Education
A Division of Rowman & Littlefield Publishers, Inc.
A wholly owned subsidary of The Rowman & Littlefield Publishing Group, Inc.
4501 Forbes Boulevard, Suite 200, Lanham, Maryland 20706
www.rowmaneducation.com

Estover Road
Plymouth PL6 7PY
United Kingdom

British Library Cataloging in Publication Information Available

Library of Congress Cataloging-in-Publication Data
Mark, Michael L.
  A concise history of American music education / Michael L. Mark.
    p. cm.
  "Published in partnership with MENC, the National Association for Music
Education."
  Includes bibliographical references.
  ISBN-13: 978-1-57886-850-6 (cloth : alk. paper)
  ISBN-10: 1-57886-850-5 (cloth : alk. paper)
  ISBN-13: 978-1-57886-851-3 (pbk. : alk. paper)
  ISBN-10: 1-57886-851-3 (pbk. : alk. paper)
  eISBN-13: 978-1-57886-905-3
  eISBN-10: 1-57886-905-6
  1. Music—Instruction and study—United States—History. I. Title.
MT3.U5M317 2008
780.71'073—dc22   2008016082

∞™ The paper used in this publication meets the minimum requirements of
American National Standard for Information Sciences—Permanence of
Paper for Printed Library Materials, ANSI/NISO Z39.48-1992.
Manufactured in the United States of America

CONTENTS

PREFACE

Musical needs differ from one society to another and from one historic period to another, but a reading of history illustrates clearly that music, and music education, have always been valued highly. This is equally true of American music education. The schools have evolved continually as they have kept up with changes in America's educational needs, and the music education profession has always responded by finding the most effective and appropriate ways to remain current, and to continue to meet the nation's musical needs.

I hope that students preparing for professional lives as music educators and those already serving in the profession will find historical insights in this book that help them value the contributions music education makes to society, that they will have a better understanding of music education's triumphs and shortcomings, and that they will be inspired by the many leaders and day-to-day music teachers who have made it what it is today.

Michael L. Mark
Baltimore, Maryland

1

MUSIC EDUCATION
IN EARLY TIMES

EARLY MUSIC EDUCATION IN EUROPE

Music educators were making important contributions to their societies long before European settlers arrived in the New World. From the earliest times, musicians and music teachers served their societies in many ways. Music was an important part of every society, and the relationship of music to the societies that sponsored it, and how music was taught, are relevant to the history of music education in America. Ancient practices in music and music education shaped the ways in which music education came to be in what is now the United States of America.

Greece and Rome

Long before Europeans discovered the New World, during the Golden Age of Greece beginning around 500 BC, Athens offered its citizens a wealth of cultural, intellectual, and athletic opportunities that allowed them to live a rich life, culturally, spiritually, and materialistically.

The purpose of education was to develop citizens capable of actively participating in Greek society. The education system emphasized music, which included poetry, and was intended to influence both body and soul. Music was important because of the many festivals, contests, and singing societies that were integral to the Greek culture. Adults were expected to participate in the musical activities.

In the first school level, boys[1] learned poetry and how to accompany themselves on the lyre. They studied music from the age of seven to

---

1. Girls did not attend school.

fourteen. The fourth century philosopher Teles described "the four chief burdens of boys" as gymnastics trainers, literary masters, painters, and music masters.

Greek students learned vocal and instrumental music. The lyre and a type of oboe called the *aulos* were essential to Greek music, and students learned to play them in school. Choral singing was especially important. Choirs were needed for religious ceremonies held by the city. The music was simple, and a master could prepare the chorus in a few rehearsals. The ceremonies, held at the times of certain feasts, were accompanied by intertribal competitions. Each tribe was represented by its choir, normally sponsored by one of its wealthy citizens. As competition intensified, some choirs began to substitute professional musicians for amateurs. This led to the decline of musical amateurism in Greek education because choral singing became too difficult for amateurs to perform. It had become complex and required technical proficiency, and by the fifth century, musical performance had become the work of specialists. The average citizen no longer participated in music, and music education declined.

Plato described his ideal state in the *Republic*, and in *Laws*.[2] Education had two basic elements—music and gymnastics. Plato's imaginary dialogue between Socrates and Glaucon in the *Republic* established a rationale for balance in education:

> There are two arts which I would say some god gave to mankind, music and gymnastics for the service of the high-spirited principle and the love of knowledge in them—not for the soul and the body except incidentally, but for the harmonious adjustment of these two principles by the proper degree of tension and relaxation of each. . . . Education in music is most sovereign, because more than anything else rhythm and harmony find their way to the innermost soul and take strongest hold upon it, bringing with them and imparting grace, if one is rightly trained. (Hamilton and Cairns 1984)

Plato believed that children must learn music to develop a perception of idealized community life and to prepare them to participate actively as responsible citizens.

Aristotle taught that students should study music to develop musical taste, not to be trained to compete with professional musicians. He

---

2. Plato's ideal education is imaginary, described in his writings. It did not exist in the real world.

wrote about "the use of music for intellectual enjoyment in leisure. . . . It is evident, then, that there is a sort of education in which parents should train their sons, not as being useful or necessary, but because it is liberal or noble."

Although music in ancient Rome had a function in civic life, the musicians were artisans who did not come from the aristocracy. Roman art and music were produced by professional artists and musicians, many of whom were slaves. Some scientifically gifted students studied music as a mathematical science in their secondary education. Music as a science was one of the seven liberal arts. The first three—grammar, logic, and rhetoric—constituted the *trivium*. The *trivium* prepared the student to be eloquent as he prepared for teaching, discourse, and preaching. The upper level of the seven liberal arts was the *quadrivium*—arithmetic, geometry, astronomy, and music. Only those who had gone beyond the *trivium* to master the *quadrivium* could know the physical and spiritual realities of the universe. This body of knowledge permitted one to penetrate the secrets of the universe and grasp the ultimate truth. University graduates went on to teach or to enter the clergy.

Boethius (475–525), the Roman statesman and scholar, wrote *De Institutione Musica*, a work that preserved Greek music theory and was valued by musicians for more than a millennium. It was studied throughout the Middle Ages as part of the *quadrivium*. It was so influential that Oxford University professors taught from it until the nineteenth century. Boethius described the study of music as follows:

> That which is most knowable is most harmonious; only quantities, magnitudes, forms, essences, are knowable, and the discipline of music concerns itself with essences consisting of related quantities; those related quantities which are easiest to know are the proportions, the essences, the most harmonious sounds.

Boethius's description of music as a mathematical science took the form of mathematical axioms and proofs. The music theorist, by studying the mathematical proportions of music, would apply reason to understand the mysteries of the universe through its proportions and harmony. The motions of the planets created pitches, and the planets moved at velocities so great that their sounds were beyond the capacity of human hearing. Music was considered a form of the all-embracing cosmic harmony that could be perceived only through the intellect, and not through the human senses (Mark and Gary 2007, 9).

The Middle Ages

There were three types of schools during the Middle Ages—monastery, cathedral, and parish. The church schools provided elementary instruction in reading, writing, and psalm singing. The cathedral and parish schools began as schools of music to prepare musicians for the church. By the end of the eighth century they taught the seven liberal arts. The great medieval musicians were trained at the cathedral and monastery schools and many became teachers in them.

Music education consisted of training in singing until musical notation was invented. Notation permitted a reasonably exact realization of the composer's musical intention. As notation developed, the emphasis in education began to shift to music reading. St. Odo of Cluny and Guido d'Arezzo were the two most important figures in the development of exact notation. Odo (c. 878–942) was a choir singer who became head of the abbey of Cluny. One of his theoretical works was *Enchiridion musices*. In it, Odo presented a systematic use of letters to represent musical pitches. It was the first time letters had been used this way, and the system became standard during the Middle Ages. The letters ran the gamut from A to G.

Guido d'Arezzo (c. 990–1050) was the most important teacher of his time. He was a choirmaster who invented another systematic method for teaching young boys to sing a melody from notation. He had them memorize the familiar hymn "Ut queant laxis" (Hymn to St. John). The beginning tone of each of the first six phrases is one note higher than the preceding one in the major scale. As a result, students were taught to recall the initial syllables of each verse (*ut*[3], *re, mi, fa, sol, la*), which are used today to teach the rudiments of music. The most critical element was the accurate location of the half step between *mi* and *fa*, which has characterized all of the many variants of the system from the eleventh century to the present. In the tenth century an unknown scribe drew a horizontal red line to represent the pitch *f* and arranged the neumes (roughly, the pitches) around the line. Later, a second line, usually yellow, was added to indicate the note C. In the eleventh century, Guido described a four-line staff that he used. Over time, it evolved into the five-line staff that is now used universally.

Written notation revolutionized the study of music. With the invention of the staff, pitches could be written exactly as they were to be performed. Sight-singing, rather than rote learning, became possible. For the

---

3. *Ut* is now what we call *do*.

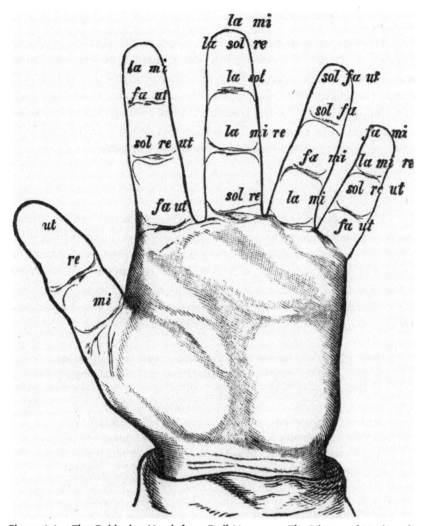

Figure 1.1.   The Guidonian Hand, from Emil Naumann, *The History of Music*, vol. 1 (London: Cassell & Co., 1888).

first time, composers wrote music for singers who could perform it as they conceived it. Notation became the major subject of study in the cathedral and court schools, and the better students went on to study polyphony and composition. This made possible the detailed notation of Renaissance polyphony and contributed to the intellectual developments that led to the Renaissance.

The Protestant Reformation

The Reformation began in 1517 when Martin Luther posted his Ninety-five Theses on the door of the castle church at Wittenberg. Luther was musical, and he advocated the teaching of singing and instrumental music. He believed that "singing good music makes a man more reasonable and well-mannered." Luther wanted children to study and enjoy music, and teachers to be musicians. The schools established under the influence of his religious teachings included music in the curriculum.

Seventeenth Century Realism

The newly emerging middle class of the seventeenth century, mostly people in mercantile and manufacturing occupations, needed to be educated. Several influential figures emerged to fill the need. John Amos Comenius of Bohemia was a leader in the new education of his time. He wrote *The Great Didactic*, in which he discussed the teaching of music and art specifically in terms of curriculum and method. He wrote about how children learn music and what they should accomplish:

> Music is especially natural to us; for as soon as we see the light we immediately sing the song of paradise, thus recalling to our memory our fall. . . . External music begins to delight children at two years of age; such as singing, rattling, and striking of musical instruments. They should therefore be indulged in this, so that their ears and minds may be soothed by concord and harmony. . . . In the third year, sacred music is to be introduced; namely, that received as a custom to sing before and after dinner, and when prayers are begun or ended. (Livingstone 1971, 144–67)

Music in German Schools

In seventeenth century Germany, elementary level students learned music principles by rote and sang by ear. Intermediate level boys progressed to music theory and part singing and composed music in class. Students in the upper level studied more advanced theory and were expected to master sight-singing and part singing. Some German schools had excellent music programs and even offered instrumental instruction. Boys sang in school and sometimes earned money by singing at weddings, funerals, and other social and civic occasions (Livingstone 1971, 144–67). German music education, especially in Prussia, was to become a model for American schools early in the nineteenth century.

EARLY MUSIC EDUCATION IN THE NEW WORLD

The Spanish Conquerors in Mexico

After Hernando Cortéz conquered Mexico for Spain in 1521, its immense wealth of natural resources promised to make Spain the wealthiest country in Europe. The Spanish conquerors needed the Native Americans to mine the silver and other minerals that lay beneath their feet. To motivate conformity, the Spanish converted the Aztecs to Christianity through the use of music.

Early in his reign, in 1523, Cortéz brought a music teacher, Pedro de Gante,[4] to Mexico to help convert the Indians. Pedro was a key figure in importing Spanish culture as Mexico's vibrant native culture was destroyed. By all accounts, Pedro was an excellent teacher. He taught the Indians to read, write, sing European music, play instruments, copy Franco-Flemish polyphony manuscripts, and build violins and organs. At night, he preached and taught Christian doctrine. This took place at least one hundred years before the Pilgrims landed on the shores of Massachusetts. Pedro's students were good musicians who loved their teacher. Many of them traveled to small villages to become teachers themselves (Stevenson 1960, 110). Pedro carried the Spanish-Catholic heritage well beyond Mexico City, and probably built as many as one hundred churches (112–13). The Spanish established a university in 1536, exactly one hundred years earlier than Harvard University was founded. Three years later a printing press was imported and the first book printed in America was an *Ordinary of the Mass*, in 1556.

In 1540, Francisco Coronado conquered the area that is now New Mexico. Like Cortéz before him, he used music to convert the Indians. The music teacher he brought from Europe was Juan de Padilla. By 1630, Spanish friars served in 25 missions with congregations of 50,000 Indians, and each had a school similar to those established by Pedro de Gante. Juan de Zumárraga, the first Franciscan bishop of Mexico City, wrote in a letter, "Indians are great lovers of music, and the religious who hear their confessions tell us that they are converted more by music than by preaching, and we can see they come from distant regions to hear it" (113).

Even before Cortéz conquered the Aztecs, music education was a part of the ancient Inca culture. There were schools for the children of the native aristocracy in what is now Peru, where music was part of the ancient curriculum. The curriculum was described by a Spanish observer:

---

4. Peter of Ghent, now Flanders, Belgium.

They taught the grounds and reasons for their system of laws, and how to apply them in governing subject peoples . . . also how to speak elegantly and correctly, how to bring up their children, and how to regulate their households. In addition, the *amautas* [masters] taught poetry and music. (Heller 1979, 23–24)

Musically talented girls from nine to fifteen years of age were placed in a nunnery where they were trained in singing and flute playing so they could entertain at banquets of the royalty and nobility.

The native Indians were so accomplished in music that it became the main tool of the Franciscans, Dominicans, Augustinians, and Jesuits as they too converted the Indians. Music was the principal subject in their schools (Britton 1958).

The Spanish conquerors converted the native populations primarily for two reasons. It is likely that many Spanish missionaries sincerely wanted to save souls, but the more earthly reason was for the wealth that the newly converted Indians were able to contribute to Spain. They were submissive to the church and to Spain, which itself was governed, to a large extent, by the laws of the church. The enslaved Indians mined their natural resources, which were then sent to Spain. That country became the wealthiest in Europe until the British defeated the Spanish Armada in 1588. Much of the wealth that was mined in Mexico can be seen today in Spanish cathedrals, which are lavishly decorated with countless artistic and religious artifacts made from the precious metals taken from American soil by the labor of enslaved Indians.

The French came to Canada with motives similar to those of the Spanish to the south, but they did not enslave the Indians. Instead, they created a fur trade in what is now Quebec. Like the Spanish, the French brought Christianity to the Indians with the use of music. A French teacher wrote from near Quebec in 1675: "The nuns of France do not sing more agreeably than some savage women here; and, as a class, all the savages have much more aptitude and inclination for singing the hymns of the Church." Music instruction was so successful that in 1668 the Iroquois received papal permission to celebrate their services, including the mass, in their native language rather than in Latin (Thwaites 1896–1901, 145). The French built missions along the Mississippi River as they moved south as far as the Gulf of Mexico. All of them had schools where singing was taught.

Many praise the conversion of native Americans because they came to accept Christianity. Others find it cruel and insensitive to people whose cultures were as venerable as those of the conquerors. It is a point that will be argued long into the future, but it is clear that by using music education as a tool for conversion, the Europeans demonstrated the power of music to influence people's beliefs and behavior.

Early Immigrants in the New World

The roots of American music education as we know it today were planted in the English colonies of New England by the Pilgrims and the Puritans. Before examining the music and education of the English settlers, we will look first at other European immigrant groups that came to America early in the Colonial period. These pious people made the arduous, dangerous journey to the New World to seek religious freedom.

William Penn held the charter to Pennsylvania, where he gave land to anyone who sought religious freedom. By 1776, more than 100,000 Anglicans, Catholics, Lutherans, Mennonites, Moravians, Pietists, and Quakers lived in Penn's colony. Many brought the sophisticated music of Europe with them, and music was an important subject in their schools. Britton wrote: "What is important to remember is that these Americans saw to it that music was taught in the first schools they organized" (Britton 1958, 198).

The religious services of many of Pennsylvania's religious sects emphasized congregational singing. Music was an important aspect of daily life for the Amish, led by Jacob Ammen, the Mennonites, led by Menno Simon, and the Moravians. The Moravians spread out to other colonies, especially North Carolina, which became a center for European-style music. In Bethlehem, Pennsylvania, the Collegium Musicum played every evening and trombone choirs play outside in the open air to this day. Despite the hardships of life in a frontier society, the Moravians composed and performed a prodigious amount of vocal and instrumental music. Music education was an integral part of Moravian education not only because it preserved their religious culture, but also because they believed that it was important to develop aesthetic sensibilities (Latrobe 1806). The purpose of music education was clarified in a Moravian publication: "That the youth should become musicians is by no means a necessary result, not even a desirable one; we would only insist that music should have its sway in the whole formation and refinement of mind and heart" (Hall 1981, 226).

MUSIC EDUCATION IN EARLY NEW ENGLAND

What we now know as American music education began with two groups of English colonists. The Pilgrims arrived in Massachusetts in 1620 and the

Puritans in 1630. Both left England to escape religious persecution as they practiced their religion freely and openly. The newly established government of the Plymouth Colony, and later the Massachusetts Bay Colony, was a theocracy, based on religious belief rather than on the democratic concept of personal freedom of choice.

The Pilgrims brought with them the *Book of Psalms* by the Reverend Henry Ainsworth. It had been written for them in Holland and published in 1612. It had 342 pages and thirty-nine psalm tunes. The tunes were written in a variety of meters so all 150 psalms could be matched to them. Ainsworth's *Book of Psalms* was the official psalter of the Plymouth Colony as late as 1692, when the settlement merged with the Massachusetts Bay Colony.

The Pilgrims and Puritans were Calvinists who believed in predestination and simplicity of worship. There were no professional musicians or musical instruments in their churches, and psalmody was the only music appropriate for worship. Their spare and severe church music consisted of biblical psalms set to folk songs. Their psalm book was *The Whole Book of Psalms,* known informally as the *Sternhold and Hopkins.* The first book printed in the English colonies was *The Whole Booke of Psalmes Faithfully Translated into English Metre. Whereunto is prefixed a discourse declaring not only the lawfulness, but also the necessity of the heavenly Ordinance of Singing Scripture Psalmes in the Churches of God*, usually referred to simply as *The Bay Psalm Book.* The book was compiled by the Committee of Thirty, a group of ministers who wanted to correct some of the inaccurate translations from the original Hebrew in the *Sternhold and Hopkins.* It was printed in Cambridge in 1639 on Stephen Day's press, which had been sent from England the previous year. *The Bay Psalm Book* went through seventy editions in thirty years. It was popular in Britain as well, where it went through eighteen editions in England and ninety-nine in Scotland.

There was another reason for the translation. The old books contained many different meters, which confused the congregations. The Ainsworth had fifteen, the *Sternhold and Hopkins* seventeen. *The Bay Psalm Book* had only six meters. The early editions had no music, probably because there were no printers in the colony who could engrave the plates. The first edition known to contain music was the ninth in 1698; it was probably the first book printed in the colonies that contained music. The book contained thirteen tunes for treble and bass. The notation was untraditional, with diamond-shaped notes and no bars. The solmization letters were printed where the text would normally have been to help the singers find the correct pitch. It was the first known example of solmization letters used in this way in America and it later became a widespread teaching device.

The musical life of the colonial South was somewhat brighter than that of the North, where psalmody was the most common type of music. Secular music was popular in the South, and there were many performances by American and European touring musicians. Charleston, South Carolina, became the musical center of America, and it drew European musicians and teachers who could earn a living there. The need for music was so great that there was a shortage of both music teachers and dancing masters. Many were itinerant, traveling from one plantation to another to teach, perform, and play the organ for church services. Unlike New England society, Southern society was stratified, and only the wealthy could participate in the rich musical life. Robert Carter, who owned a plantation in Northern Neck, Virginia, is an example. He had a pianoforte, harpsichord, guitar, violin, German flutes, and an armonica (one of Benjamin Franklin's inventions). There was a school on the plantation for his two sons, five daughters, and one nephew. It had a rigid daily schedule:

7:00–8:00 AM	School
9:30	Breakfast
9:30–12:00	School
12:00 PM	Play
2:00	Dinner
3:30–5:00	School
8:00	Supper

Carter hired a music master to teach the girls piano and harpsichord, and he himself taught them guitar. The children were excused from some school time on Tuesdays and Thursdays to practice. Dancing was also important, and a boy was flogged for skipping dancing school.

Parents who were not so wealthy sometimes would band together to build schoolhouses and hire schoolmasters. It was not unusual for girls to be sent to boarding schools where music and dancing were generally offered (Spruill 1972, 102, 196). Most Southerners did not have the opportunity to learn music in school, and they welcomed the Northern singing schools as they began to spread to the South.

Education in New England

Education in New England was profoundly different from that of the southern colonies. The New Englanders believed in universal education. The Massachusetts Bay Colony passed laws in 1642, 1647, and 1648 that required towns to have schools. The *Massachusetts School Law of 1648* even specified what was to be taught:

> For as much as the good education of children is of singular behoof and benefit to any Common-wealth; and whereas many parents and masters are too indulgent and negligent of their duty in that kinde. It is therefore ordered that the Select men of everie town, in the severall precincts and quarters where they dwell, shall have a vigilant eye over their brethren and neighbours to see, first that none of them shall suffer so much barbarism in any of their families as not to indeavor to teach by themselves or others, their children and apprentices so much learning as may inable them perfectly to read the english tongue, and knowledge of the Capital lawes; upon penalties of twentie shillings for each neglect therein. Also that all masters of families doe once a week (at the least) catechize their children and servants in the grounds and principles of Religion. . . . And further that all parents and masters do breed and bring up their children and apprentices in some honest lawful calling, labour or employment, either in husbandry, or some other trade profitable for themselves, and the Common-wealth, if they will not or can not train them up in learning to fit them for higher employments. (Cohen 1974, 394–95)

The Connecticut, Plymouth, and New Hampshire legislatures passed similar laws within a few decades. These laws focused on vocational and religious training. Music was not included; instead, it was taught privately in singing schools. There were no such laws in the South, where education was a private matter.

THE NEW ENGLAND ROOTS OF
AMERICAN MUSIC EDUCATION

The Pilgrims' journey on the *Mayflower* ended at Plymouth in 1620, and the Puritans arrived ten years later. Conditions were very different from what they had known in Europe. They had to learn basic survival skills—finding food, creating shelter and clothing—that required virtually all of their attention and time. The survival skills they learned came at the expense of some cultural practices that had been important in their old lives, but which had to be put off until they were established firmly enough to begin enjoying them again in the New World. The music of their church service was important to them, but they could not give it much attention until they had the basic necessities of life.

The New England theocratic authorities were concerned with the declining quality of music in the church service. They believed that congregations needed to be educated in music. It was in New England that a formal system of music education for the masses developed. Ironically, mass music education emerged from a fundamental difference in the way congregations sang psalm tunes.

Opposing Practices in Psalm-tune Singing:
The Regular Way and the Old Way

Two methods of singing psalm tunes had been imported from the Old World. The Regular Way consisted of singing by note, or reading music. The Old Way, or "lining out," originated in England for parishioners who could not read music. It also became a tradition there and in the New World, where most people were musically illiterate. Each line of a psalm was read by a deacon, or precentor, who gave the starting pitch and led the congregational singing. The congregation repeated the line, and the process was begun again for each succeeding line. Calvinist congregations practiced lining out because worshipers were expected to hear, understand, and sing the biblical words (Temperley 1981). Lining out was a common practice in seventeenth century churches and still exists in some Southern Baptist churches.

The quality of church music declined sharply during the first few generations in the New England colonies. Often, the tune was in a key that was too high or too low, the tempo dragged, and the precentor would change the tune and add embellishments. Tunes were sometimes unrecognizable. Most congregations only knew a few tunes, and the same ones were sung differently from one congregation to another and from one person to another. The Reverend Cotton Mather wrote in 1721, "It has been found . . . in some of our congregations, that in length of time, their singing has degenerated into an odd noise, that has more of what we want a name for, than any Regular Singing in it" (Morse 1888, 21).

The quality of church singing in the Old World was not much better. Doctor Burney, Samuel Johnson's friend, wrote in his *History of Music* (1789) of church singing in England, or what he called "bawling out":

> The greatest blessing to lovers of music in a parish church is to have an
> organ in it sufficiently powerful to render the voices of the clerk & those
> who join in his outcry wholle inaudible. Indeed all reverence for the
> psalms seems to be lost by the wretched manner in which they are sung.

Dr. Millar Patrick wrote of lining out in Scotland:

> Singing of the psalms, inexpressibly dreary, was made worse by the importation from England of the practice of "lining"—the precentor reading or intoning each line before it was sung. Such a practice, necessary where the people had few or no psalters or where they were in general illiterate, was absurd in Scotland, where the people could read; yet it established itself so firmly in favor that in some cases congregations suffered serious secessions when it began to be abandoned. (Millar 1932, 43)

Despite its shortcomings, lining out persisted because worshipers believed it to be a tradition that pleased God. Eventually, many New England ministers became so discouraged with the music that they began to advocate for music instruction to teach their congregations to read music. The ministers were insistent in their sermons and writings. Reverend John Tufts of Newbury, Massachusetts, was a leader in the new movement. His sermons disparaged musical illiteracy and he wrote the first American textbook to solve the problem. He was the most significant figure in American music education until the 1820s, when Lowell Mason began a new movement and changed the course of music education. Tufts's advocacy led to the *singing school*, which influenced American music and music education for over a hundred years. His book, *An Introduction to The Singing of Psalm-Tunes* (1721), was the first practical attempt to improve the situation. The first known reference to the work is in a 1721 newspaper advertisement placed by the publisher:

> A small Book containing 20 Psalm Tunes, with Directions how to Sing them, contrived in the most easy Method ever yet Invented, for the ease of Learners, whereby even Children, or People of the meanest Capacities, may come to Sing them by Rule, may serve as an Introduction to a more compleat Treatise of Singing, which will speedily be published. To be Sold by Samuel Gerrish Bookseller; near the Brick Church in Cornhill. Price 6d. (Lowens 1954, 89–90)

The "more compleat Treatise of Singing" probably refers to Thomas Walter's *Grounds and Rules of Musick Explained* (Boston, 1721), which was also announced by Gerrish in the *Boston News Letter* of May 15 and 21, 1721.

The title page of the third edition (1723) of Tufts's *Introduction to the Singing of Psalm Tunes* read:

An introduction to the art of singing psalm-tunes; in the most plain and easy method ever yet made known. Or, a collection of the best psalm-tunes in two parts, fitted to the meanest capacity. First contrived by the Reverend Mr. Tufts. The third edition. With an addition of the basses of the tunes printed from a copper plate correctly engraven. Boston: Printed by T. Fleet, for Samuel Gerrish, near the Brick Meeting-House in Cornhill. 1723.

"The Publisher's Preface" expressed optimism about the success of the book:

> THERE has been of late a wonderful, and laudable Inclination in multitudes of People, both Old and Young, to learn to Sing according to the Rules of Music; and the Reformation that has been already made, begins to be visible in many Congregations, both in this Town, and many Towns in the Country. . . . It is plain that the following easy Method of singing the Psalm Tunes, has been greatly Instrumental of promoting this good Work; it has answer'd its End far beyond what was first expected. (Finney 1966, 166)

Tufts invented his own system for teaching music reading. He substituted the first letters of the four solmization syllables—*Fa, Sol, La,* and *Mi*—on the staff in place of the traditional round notes. The four syllables represented the seven notes of the scale. The practice of singing with four syllables was known as *fasola* singing. The letters represented pitches by their placement on the appropriate lines and spaces of the musical staff. *Fa, sol, la* were sung for the first three tones of the scale and *fa* was then sung one half step higher than the *la* for the fourth tone. *Sol* and *la* followed for steps five and six, and *mi* was used for the seventh tone—the leading tone one half step below the tonic *fa,* that began the new octave. Identifying the keynote by the position of *mi* became a standard technique taught by singing masters, who adopted the practice both in American and British schools (Mark and Gary 2007, 73).

Tufts's rhythm notation changed as well. He substituted punctuation marks for flags. A period signified a half note, a colon a whole note, and a quarter note had no punctuation. Although his kind of letter notation had been used earlier in Europe, it is likely that Tufts reinvented it. The system was not widely accepted, but it was an important model for later systems.

The appendix to *An Introduction to the Singing of Psalm Tunes* contained instruction in the rudiments of music, for tuning the voice, musical notation, intervals, scales, clefs, and meter signatures. The book became the

DIRECTIONS

For Singing

The TUNES which follow.

THE Letters F, S, L, M, mark'd on the
several Lines and Spaces in the following Tunes, stand for these Syllables, viz. *Fa,
Sol, La, Mi,* and are to shew you,

I. The Distance of the Notes one from another in each Tune, or to give you the true Pitch
of every Note. Therefore observe, From *Mi* to
Fa, and from *La* to *Fa* ascending ; or, from
Fa to *La,* and from *Fa* to *Mi* descending, are
but half Notes, or Semitones. From *Fa* to *Sol,*
from *Sol* to *La,* and from *La* to *Mi* ascending ;
or, from *Mi* to *La,* from *La* to *Sol,* and from
Sol to *Fa* descending, are whole Notes, or
Tones. *Mi* is the Principal Note, and the Notes
rising gradually above *Mi,* are *Fa, Sol, La, Fa,
Sol, La,* and then *Mi* again : And the Notes
fall-

Figure 1.2. Directions for reading Tufts's distinctive notation from *An Introduction to the Singing of Psalm Tunes.* Reproduction from the collections of the Library of Congress.

prototype for numerous other books published throughout the eighteenth century.

Another reformer, Reverend Thomas Symmes, wrote a pamphlet entitled *The Reasonableness of Regular Singing, or Singing by Note* (1720), subtitled *An Essay to revive the true and ancient mode of Singing psalm-tunes according to the pattern of our New-England psalm-books.* He described singing by note as follows:

> Now singing by note is giving every note its proper pitch, and turning the voice in its proper place, and giving to every note its true length and sound. Whereas, the usual way varies much from this. In it, some notes are sung too high, others too low, and most too long, and many turnings or flourishings with the voice are made where they should not be, and some are wanting where they should have been. (Symmes 1720, 18)

Reverend Thomas Walter of Roxbury, Massachusetts, also published a manual on singing the Regular Way. His book, *The Grounds and Rules of Music Explained or An Introduction to the Art of Singing by Note,* was published in Boston in 1721.[5] The subtitle read *An Introduction to the Art of Singing by Note. Fitted to the Meanest Capacities.* Walter wrote in the introduction:

> Once the tunes were sung according to the rules of music but are now miserably tortured, and twisted, and quavered, in some churches, into an horrid Medley of confused and disorderly Noise. . . . Our tunes are, for Want of a Standard to appeal to in all our Singing, left to the Mercy of every unskilful Throat to chop and alter, twist and change, according to their infinitely divers and no less odd Humours and Fancies . . . have observed in many places, one man is upon this note while another is upon the note before him, which produces something so hideous and disorderly as is beyond expression bad.

Justifying the change to the Regular Way, he wrote: "Somebody or other did compose our tunes, and did they, think ye compose them by rule or by rote? If the latter how come they are prick'd [written] down in our Psalm books?" *The Grounds and Rules of Music Explained* used conventional notation, probably because Walter expected it to be more readily accepted than a new and unfamiliar system like Tufts's. The book had twenty-four tunes in three parts and the introduction included "Some brief and very plain Instructions for Singing by Note."

---

5. The book was printed by James Franklin during the time that his brother, Benjamin, was an apprentice in his shop.

Some congregations resisted the Regular Way and others accepted it over time. The change began in the cities, where people had more exposure to European musical traditions and standards. The Old Way persisted in rural areas much longer but eventually the conservative country people began to reform as well. The New England ministers' reforms influenced American education far into the future. Their work profoundly influenced the establishment of a formal system of music education to provide music instruction to the masses.

The Singing School Movement

Reverend Thomas Symmes asked in 1723:

> Would it not greatly tend to promote singing of psalms if singing schools were promoted? . . . Where would be the difficulty, or what the disadvantages, if people who want skill in singing, would procure a skillful person to instruct them, and meet two or three evenings in the week, from five or six o'clock to eight, and spend their time in learning to sing? (Chase 1987, 27)

Symmes and other ministers were strong advocates, and singing schools began to be established. The movement toward the Regular Way gained momentum quickly. As early as 1722, there was a Society for Promoting Regular Singing in Boston, where Reverend Walter gave a lecture entitled "The sweet Psalmist of Israel: A Sermon Preach'd at the Lecture held in Boston, by the Society for promoting Regular and Good Singing, and for reforming the Depravations and Debasement, our Psalmody labours under, In Order to introduce the proper and true Old Way of Singing" (Chase 1987, 27).

The singing schools provided a livelihood for numerous singing masters, many of whom were also composers. The schools became a tradition in which singing masters held classes in communities to teach people to sing by note. The masters helped people improve church music while providing a welcome social opportunity at the same time. The singing school gave people a place to interact with their friends and neighbors. Many students were young adults who were pleased to have an opportunity to socialize. Birge quotes former singing school students as they reminisced about their experiences in his *History of Public School Music in the United States*. Henry Perkins wrote: "Those were halcyon days. We not only sang every exercise, tune, and anthem to do, re, mi . . . but at the close . . . we escorted the prettiest girl, to our way of thinking, home." Secular music gradually was added to the tune books as the singing schools satisfied both religious and worldly purposes.

The singing master would advertise his singing school with a newspaper announcement or by posting broadsides (posters) that told the amount of tuition charged, the schedule and place of classes, and other necessary information. The school normally took place in a home or a classroom (Birge 1966, 12). Classes usually met in the evening from one to five times each week and lasted from a few weeks to six months.

The singing school that ended with a concert by the students and a sermon by a minister was called a singing lecture. It was called a singing assembly if there was no sermon. The itinerant singing master would then go on to another community for another singing school. Some singing masters were Yankee peddlers as well, carrying merchandise to sell along the way or in the new community. Some provided other services, like wheelwright, carpenter, mason, or tanner. The singing master might spend part of the year working at home at another occupation and travel part of the year, or he might travel all the time. The students would buy their tune books from the singing master. The books contained instructions for reading music and a collection of psalms, hymns, and other music to be sung in class. Much of the music was composed by singing masters, sometimes by the one selling the book.

Musical tastes began to change as the industrial revolution brought more and more country people to jobs in the cities, and as the cities absorbed European immigrants throughout the eighteenth and nineteenth centuries. Interest in psalmody and church hymns declined, and eventually, urban Americans came to disdain it, regarding singing school music as unsophisticated and unrefined, the music of country people. Singing schools had existed in all rural areas of the country but they continued longer in the South because there were no public schools to replace them, as in the North. The development of choral societies also competed with the singing schools. The singing schools persisted, however, and contributed to American cultural life for two centuries, from the early 1700s to the early 1900s.

The singing school was an evening or night school. Evening schools were organized to provide instruction in subjects not offered in the public school curriculum. Students attended evening schools voluntarily and at their own expense to learn subjects like languages, surveying, dancing, sewing, and handicrafts. When the subjects were proven to be of lasting interest, some were absorbed into the public school curriculum (Britton 1961, 77–79). People no longer had to attend singing schools to learn to read music and sing. This was the primary reason for the decline of the singing schools in the latter half of the nineteenth century. More and more public schools began to offer free music instruction in competition with the singing schools.

The singing schools made public school music possible. The first teaching methods and the first public school music teachers came from the singing schools. It is unlikely that public schools would have adopted music programs if not for the well-established singing school tradition of teaching music to the public.

The Tune Books

The singing school texts, "tune books" or "open-enders," were oblong in shape. About 1,400 of them were published, many with long, laborious titles. An example was titled *The Delights of Harmony; or, Norfolk Compiler, Being a new collection of psalm tunes, hymns and anthems; with a variety of set pieces. From the most approved American and European authors. Likewise, the necessary rules of psalmody made easy. The whole particularly designed for the use of singing schools and musical societies in the United States. By Stephen Jenks . . . Dedham, Mass . . . 1805.*

The tune books were both instructional texts and collections of choral music. They included an appendix that presented the rudiments of music. Rudiments began to be included with the publication of John Tufts's *Introduction* and Thomas Walter's *The Grounds and Rules of Musick Explained.* Basic music reading instruction was presented in some tune books; others presented elaborate, complex instructions, sometimes even venturing into advanced music theory. By the end of the nineteenth century, some tune books included complete lesson plans.

The pedagogical sections of the tune books began to change in the early part of the nineteenth century when the principles of the Swiss educator Johann Pestalozzi's influence began to be felt in American education. Pestalozzian principles were adapted for music instruction. These principles were new to tune books and they changed the nature of music instruction in the United States.

When Lowell Mason began to apply Pestalozzian principles to a teaching method, he developed a new format that affected the teaching of music throughout the country. In the ninth edition of the *Boston Handel and Haydn Society's Collection of Church Music,* he presented the instructional material in the music lessons, rather than as separate expository material. He also included questions for the teacher to ask students and the responses to be expected. In 1830, Elam Ives divided instruction into three "departments"—rhythm,

Figure 1.3. Page 47 of Joseph Funk, *A Compilation of Genuine Church Music, Comprising a Variety of Metres, All Harmonized for Three Voices, Together with a Copious Elucidation of the Science of Vocal Music* (Harrisonburg, VA: Joseph Funk & Sons, 1847).

pitch, and dynamics—and Mason began to use these headings in 1839. The new pedagogy made students active learners by mixing the instructional material with musical exercises (Perrin 1970, 67).

Mason added exercises to the pedagogical section in the *Modern Psalmist* (1839). After that, virtually every new tune book included exercises interspersed with the texts. The question and answer section evolved into review questions, and the presentation of musical elements was solidified into rhythm, melody, and dynamics. These changes created a new format for tune books (Perrin 1970, 68).

Innovative Systems of Notation

Tune-book authors invented many new notation systems to simplify music reading. The most successful was shape notes, which consisted of a different shape for each of the four syllables. Singers knew the pitch by the shape of the note rather than by its placement on the staff. This notation was also referred to as "patent notes," or derisively as "buckwheat notes." William Little and William Smith were the first to use shape notes in *The Easy Instructor* (1798), followed by Andrew Law's *The Art of Singing*. *The Easy Instructor* was traditional in everything but the shapes of the notes. Little and Smith used a triangular note head for *fa*, a round note for *sol*, a square for *la*, and a diamond for *mi* (Mark and Gary 2007, 84). The shapes conformed to the then-current Anglo-American solmization system, in which major scales began and ended on *fa*. Minor scales began on *la*. Teachers began to favor a system of seven different shapes, one for each note of the scale, as Pestalozzian changes started to influence tune books.

Many versions of shape notes were published throughout the nineteenth century and even into the twentieth century, especially in the South. Shape notes came to be associated with rural people. Eventually, traditional notation triumphed and shape notes were abandoned. Even though they were the object of derision, shape notes helped people learn to read music and a proven educational tool was lost.

The Music of the Tune Books

The tune books included several types of pieces, mostly psalm and hymn tunes. The liveliest form was the fuging tune, in two parts. The first section was homophonic and ended on the tonic or dominant; the second featured imitative melodies of up to two measures and was repeated, making an ABB form. It was not actually a fugue, just a simple imitative section by relatively untrained composers. The fuging tune was created in England and was loved in New England. In *Poganuc People* (1879), Harriet Beecher Stowe described a scene around 1820 in which Billings's tune "Majesty" was sung:

> If there were pathos and power and solemn splendour in the rhythmic movements of the churchly chants, there was a grand, wild freedom, an energy of motion in the old "fuguing" tunes of that day that well expressed the heart of a people courageous in combat and unshaken in endurance. The Church Chant is like the measure motion of the mighty sea in calm weather but those old "fuguing" tunes were like that same ocean aroused by stormy winds, when deep calleth unto deep in tempestuous confusion, out of which at last is evolved union and harmony. It was a music suggestive of the strife, commotion, the battle-cries of a transition period of society, struggling onward towards dimly seen ideals of peace and order. Whatever the trained musician might say of such a tune as old *Majesty*, no person of imagination and sensibility could hear it well rendered by a large choir without deep emotion. . . . And when the Doctor rose to his sermon the music had done its work upon his audience in exalting their mood to listen with sympathetic ears to whatever he might have to say.

Other musical forms were the *set piece,* the *anthem,* and the *sentence.* The music was simple, flowing, and rhythmically strong. It featured modal progressions, unusual dissonances, open fifths, and parallel fifths and octaves. Most of the texts were religious, and more came from the poetry of Isaac Watts than from any other author.

William Billings (1746–1800)

William Billings was the best known of the Yankee composers. Billings apprenticed himself to a tanner around the age of fourteen and worked at that trade for most of his life. He was lame in one leg, had one eye, a deformed arm and a harsh voice, and was addicted to snuff. He was married and had at least six children. In the language of his day, he was "without any address," meaning that he lacked social grace. His enthusiasm for music was unbounded and he often exclaimed his love for it. Billings joyfully described the fuging tune:

> There is more variety in one piece of fuging music than in twenty pieces of plain song. . . . Each part seems determined by dint of harmony and strength of accent, to drown his competitor in an ocean of harmony,

and while each part is thus mutually striving for mastery, and sweetly contending for victory, the audience are most luxuriously entertained, and exceedingly delighted; in the mean time, their minds are surprisingly agitated, and extremely fluctuated. . . . Now the solemn bass demands their attention, now the manly tenor, now the lofty counter, now the volatile treble, now here, now there, now here again O enchanting! O ecstatic. Push on, push on ye sons of harmony. (from *The Continental Harmony*, 1794)

Billings had no formal schooling after the age of fourteen, when his father died. He was a gifted musician and probably had music lessons from a local choirmaster. He also studied Tans'urs *Musical Grammar*. One of his personal characteristics was supreme self-confidence, which left him unconcerned about his lack of musical training. He wrote:

Perhaps it may be expected by some, that I should say something concerning Rules for Composition; to these I answer that Nature is the best Dictator, for all the hard, dry, studied rules that ever was prescribed, will not enable any person to form an air . . . It must be Nature, Nature must lay the Foundation, Nature must inspire the Thought. . . . For my own Part, as I don't think myself confin'd to any Rules for composition, laid down by any that went before me, neither should I think (were I to pretend to lay down Rules) that any one who came after me were any ways obligated to adhere to them, any further than they should think proper; so in fact, I think it best for every Composer to be his own Carver. (Billings 1770, 19)

Billings wrote psalm settings, hymn settings, anthems, canons for chorus, and patriotic songs. One of his most memorable compositions was "Chester," which was included in *The New England Psalm Singer* (1770). His second book, *The Singing Master's Assistant* (1778), contained "Chester" with new patriotic verses. With its stirring new text, "Chester" became the marching and battle song of George Washington's Continental Army during the Revolutionary War.

Billings included "Rules for Regulating a Singing-School" in *The Singing Master's Assistant*. Having conducted singing schools himself, he was aware of the logistical and disciplinary problems faced by singing masters. He wrote:

As the well being of every society depends in a great measure upon GOOD ORDER. I here present you with some general rules, to be observed in a Singing-School.

1st. Let the society be first formed, and articles signed by every indi-vidual; and all those who are under age, should apply to their parents, masters or guardians to sign for them: the house should be provided, and every necessary for the school should be procured, before the arrival of the Master, to prevent his being unnecessarily detained.

2d. The Members should be very punctual in attending at a certain, hour, or minute, as the master shall direct, under the penalty of a small fine, and if the master should be delinquent, his fine to be double the sum laid upon the scholars—Said fine to be appropriated to the use of the school, in procuring wood, candies, &tc.

3d. All the scholars should submit to the judgment of the master, respecting the part they are to sing; and if he should think fit to remove them from one part to another, they are not to contradict, or cross him in his judgment; but they would do well to suppose it is to answer some special purpose; because it is orally impossible for him to proportion the parts properly, until he has made himself acquainted with the strength and fitness of the pupil's voices.

Billings's fourth point cautions against unnecessary conversation, whisper-ing, or laughing, which he considered to be impolite (McKay and Craw-ford 1973, 16–17).

Other well-known composers of the era were Supply Belcher, Daniel Read, Oliver Holden, Justin Morgan, Andrew Law, and Jeremiah Ingalls.

Black Americans and the Singing Schools

Black singing masters and singing school students were part of the singing school movement. Cotton Mather organized the Society of Ne-groes, who were instructed in singing as early as 1674. In 1854, the Rever-end Hanks conducted a singing school for blacks in a Wilmington, North Carolina, church with a mixed congregation and at the same time a singing school for whites in a church with a white congregation (Ring 1980, 146). Newport Gardner (c. 1746–1826) was a slave of the Gardner family. He probably studied music with Andrew Law in Providence, Rhode Island, in 1783, and then conducted his own singing school in Newport, Rhode Island. He was described in an 1830 book by John Ferguson:

Newport Gardner . . . early discovered to his owner very superior pow-ers of mind. He taught himself to read, after receiving a few lessons on the elements of written language. He taught himself to sing, after receiv-ing a very trivial initiation into the rudiments of music. He became so well acquainted with the science and art of music, that he composed a large number of tunes, some of which have been highly approved by musical amateurs, and was for a long time the teacher of a very numerously-attended singing school in Newport. (Southern 1971, 80–81)

Gardner obtained his freedom in 1791 and was made a deacon of the Congregational Church.

According to Andrew Law, "Frank the Negro" directed a singing school in New York City in 1746 with as many as forty scholars (Southern 1971, 80–81). There were undoubtedly other black singing masters as well.

The Decline of the Singing School

The music of the singing school was a popular early American heritage. As the economy grew and wealth began to accumulate, many people acquired the means to enjoy European culture in America. A new reform movement began to develop in opposition to the New England style. Andrew Law, who had composed for years in the New England style, wrote that as his knowledge of the "sublime and beautiful compositions of the great Masters of Music had grown, he sought to substitute serious, animated, and devout music for that lifeless and insipid, or that frivolous and frolicsome succession and combination of sounds" that had been created by the New England composers (Grashel 1981, 66). Elias Mann wrote in his tune book (1807) that he had included "none of those wild fugues, and rapid and confused movements, which have so long been the disgrace of congregational psalmody."

The word "science" came to describe the new and desirable music that should replace the old. New England music became "unscientific" because it did not conform to European music, the new norm. Throughout the nineteenth century, the Yankee music was reviled and disdained by music critics and music historians. In 1848, Augusta Brown wrote an article for *The Musician and Intelligencer* of Cincinnati that exemplified the widespread condescension toward Yankee music. She wrote:

> The most mortifying feature and grand cause of the low estate of scientific music among us, is the presence of common Yankee singing schools, so called. We of course can have no allusion to the educated professors of vocal music, from New England, but to the genuine Yankee singing masters, who profess to make an accomplished amateur in one month, and a regular professor of music, not in seven years, but in one quarter, and at the expense, to the initiated person, usually one dollar. Hundreds of country idlers, too lazy or too stupid for farmers or

mechanics, "go to singing school for a spell," get diplomas from others scarcely better qualified than themselves, and then with their brethren, the far famed "Yankee Peddlars," itinerant to all parts of the land, to corrupt the taste and pervert the judgment of the unfortunate people who, for want of better, have to put up with them.

The decline of the singing schools is also attributed to the growing belief that the public schools should include music in the curriculum. Lowell Mason, a highly respected champion of music in public education, was instrumental in replacing unscientific practices with the cultivated European tradition. As more and more public school systems throughout the country adopted music as a tax-supported curricular subject, the need for singing schools declined. Many of the singing masters eventually abandoned their singing school careers and became music teachers in public schools.

TOPICS FOR THOUGHT AND DISCUSSION

1. Why has music education been important to the various societies it has served throughout Western history?
2. In what ways did music education earlier in Western history influence music education in the New World?
3. Discuss the forced conversion of the natives of Mexico and other Latin countries to Christianity.
4. What did the Pilgrims and Puritans have to overcome before they could give more attention to the music of their church service?
5. Why did the Regular Way of singing in the church service eventually win out over the Old Way?
6. Why did music education develop so differently in the Northern and the Southern colonies?
7. Why were the singing schools so popular?
8. Discuss the gradual extinction of shape notes and the acceptance of traditional musical notation.
9. Discuss the reasons for the decline of the singing schools.

REFERENCES

Billings, William. 1770. *New England Psalm Singer*. Boston: Edes & Gill.
Birge, Edward Bailey. 1966. *History of Public School Music in the United States*. Washington, DC: Music Educators National Conference.

Bower, C. 1966. "Boethius's *The Principles of Music,* an Introduction, Translation, and Commentary." PhD dissertation, George Peabody College for Teachers.

Britton, Allen P. 1958. "Music in Early American Public Education: A Historical Critique." *Basic Concepts in Music Education,* pt. 1. Chicago: National Society for the Study of Education, University of Chicago Press.

———. 1961. "The Singing School Movement in the United States." *Report of the Eighth Congress of the International Musicological Society,* vol. 1.

Carpenter, Nan Cooke. Spring 1953. "The Study of Music at the University of Oxford in the Middle Ages (to 1450)." *Journal of Research in Music Education.*

Chase, Gilbert. 1987. *America's Music.* 2nd ed. New York: McGraw-Hill.

———. 1988. *America's Music.* 4th ed. New York: McGraw-Hill.

Cohen, Sol, ed. 1974. *Education in the United States: A Documentary History.* Vol. I. New York: Random House.

Finney, Theodore M. 1966. "The Third Edition of Tufts' *Introduction to the Art of Singing Psalm-Tunes.*" *Journal of Research in Music Education* 14 (fall).

Grashel, John W. 1981. "The Gamut and Solmization in Early British and American Texts." *Journal of Research in Music Education* 29 (1): 63–70.

Grout, Donald J., and Claude Palisca. 1988. *A History of Western Music.* 4th ed. New York: Norton.

Hall, Harry H. Fall 1981. "Moravian Music Education in America, ca. 1750 to ca. 1830," *Journal of Research in Music Education* 29.

Hamilton, Edith, and Huntington Cairns, eds. 1984. *The Collected Dialogues of Plato.* Bollingen series 71, reprinted by Princeton University Press.

Harrison, Frank L. 1992. "The Musical Impact of Exploration and Cultural Encounter." In *Musical Repercussions of 1492: Encounters in Text and Performance,* ed. Carol E. Robertson. Washington, DC: Smithsonian Institution.

Heller, George. 1979. "Fray Pedro de Gante Pioneer American Music Educator." *Journal of Research in Music Education* 27.

Klein, Nancy Kirkland. 1990. "Music and Music Education in the Shaker Societies of America." *Bulletin of Historical Research in Music Education* 11 (winter).

Kresteff, A. D. 1962. "Musica Disciplina and Music Sonora." *Journal of Research in Music Education* 10.

Latrobe, C. I., ed. 1806. *Hymn Tunes Sung in the Church of the United Brethren.* London: The Editor.

Livingstone, Ernest F. 1954. "The Study of Music at the University of Paris in the Middle Ages." *Journal of Research in Music Education* 2 (fall).

———. 1955. "Music in the Medieval Universities." *Journal of Research in Music Education* 3.

———. 1958. *Music in Medieval and Renaissance Universities.* Norman, OK: University of Oklahoma Press.

———. 1971. "The Place of Music in German Education around 1600. *Journal of Research in Music Education* 12.

Lowens, Irving. 1954. "John Tufts' *Introduction to the Singing of Psalm-Tunes* (1721–1744): The First American Music Textbook." *Journal of Research in Music Education* 2 (fall).

Mark, Michael L. 2007. *Source Readings in Music Education History*. New York: Schirmer.

Mark, Michael L., and Charles L. Gary. 2007. *A History of American Music Education*. New York: Routledge.

Mather, Cotton. 1721. *The Accomplished Singer.* "Intended for the assistance of all that sing psalms with grace in their hearts, but more particularly to accompany the laudable endeavours of those who are learning to sing by Rule, and seeking to preserve a REGULAR SINGING in the Assemblies of the Faithful."

McKay, David P., and Richard Crawford. 1973. "The Performance of William Billings' Music." *Journal of Research in Music Education* 21 (4).

Millar, Patrick. 1932. *Manual of Church Praise*. Edinburgh: Church of Scotland. In Irving Lowens, "John Tufts' *Introduction to the Singing of Psalm-Tunes* (1721–1744)."

Miller, Samuel D. 1973. "Guido d'Arezzo: Medieval Musician and Educator." *Journal of Research in Music Education* 21 (fall).

Morse, Edward S. 1888. *Olden-Time Music: A Compilation from Newspapers and Books*. Boston: Ticknor & Company.

Perrin, Phil D. 1970. "Pedagogical Philosophy, Methods, and Materials of American Tunebook Introductions: 1801–1860." *Journal of Research in Music Education* 18 (spring).

Ring, Nancy. 1980. "Black Musical Activities in Ante-bellum Wilmington, North Carolina." *Black Perspectives in Music* 8.

Southern, Eileen. 1971. *The Music of Black Americans*. New York: Norton.

Spruill, Julia Cherry. 1972. *Women's Life and Work in the Southern Colonies*. New York: Norton.

Stevenson, Robert M. 1960. "Music Instruction in Inca Land." *Journal of Research in Music Education* 8 (fall).

Symmes, Thomas. 1720. "The Reasonableness of Regular Singing, or Singing by Note." Boston: B. Green, for Samuel Gerrish. In *William Billings of Boston*. Princeton: Princeton University Press, 1975.

Tarry, Joe E. 1973. "Music in the Educational Philosophy of Martin Luther." *Journal of Research in Music Education* 21 (winter).

Temperley, Nicholas. 1981. "The Old Way of Singing: Its Origins and Development." *Journal of the American Musicological Society* 34 (fall).

Temperley, Nicholas, and Charles G. Manns. 1983. *Fuging Tunes in the Eighteenth Century*. Detroit: Detroit Studies in Music Bibliography, 49.

Thwaites, Reuben G., ed. 1896–1901. *The Jesuit Relations and Allied Documents*. Vol. 60. Cleveland, OH: Burrows Brothers.

2

MUSIC: A CURRICULAR SUBJECT

THE PESTALOZZIAN EDUCATION
REFORM MOVEMENT

American educators, being relatively new to public education, looked for models of successful methods in other countries. The most influential teacher of children at that time was the Swiss educator Johann Heinrich Pestalozzi, whose theories influenced education throughout Europe as well as in the United States.

Johann Heinrich Pestalozzi (1746–1827)

Pestalozzi's theories changed the way people viewed elementary education and the relationship between children and adults at a time when American educators had little experience with education innovations. Pestalozzi was committed to social reform throughout his life. He believed that education was the only means to elevate the social and economic status of impoverished Swiss peasants in a feudal society, who had little if any opportunity to improve their lives. Their misery distressed Pestalozzi, and he wanted to give them dignity through education. He replaced strict discipline and the traditional memorization teaching method with one based on love and understanding of the individual child.

The Fundamentals of Pestalozzian Education

Pestalozzi believed that the purpose of education was to prepare people to achieve their highest potential at the level of their station in life, and he advocated reforms that would allow pupils to relate education to life activities. The purposes of Pestalozzi's education reform effort were morality and citizenship; the education of children therefore must elevate their three major capacities—the moral, physical, and mental faculties.[1] These three goals influenced the Boston School Committee as it considered whether to adopt music as a curricular subject.

Pestalozzian Music Instruction

Pestalozzi valued music but he did not teach it, nor was it part of his education system. Michael Traugott Pfeiffer and Hans Georg Nägeli incorporated Pestalozzian pedagogical principles in an 1812 music method entitled *Gesangbildungslehre nach Pestalozzischen Grundsätzen, Pädagogisch Begründet von Michael Traugott Pfeiffer*, Methodisch Bearbeitet von Hans Georg Nägeli in 1812 (Efland 1983, 171–72). Nägeli, a colleague and disciple of Pestalozzi, had organized singing classes in Swiss schools because he believed that group singing would promote social unity and religious values, and would stimulate a desire for good music. Nägeli also wanted uneducated adults to spend their leisure time in worthwhile pursuits that would enrich their lives and promote social values. Much of the adult Swiss population was uneducated and there was little organized musical life outside of the large towns. In 1805, Nägeli formed the Zürich Singinstitut, a musical organization consisting of a mixed choir and a children's choir. The Singinstitut's public performances demonstrated how well a musical organization could serve the community (Raynor 1878, 89). Switzerland and other German-speaking countries adopted a singing method based on Pestalozzian principles between 1810 and 1830. The German state of Prussia established the first national system of music education based on Pestalozzian principles.

The Pestalozzian Influence on American Music Education

William Channing Woodbridge was one of the first Americans to suggest music as a regular part of the public school curriculum. On August 24, 1830, Woodbridge delivered a speech in Representatives Hall in Boston to the American Institute of Instruction entitled "On Vocal Music as a Branch of Common Education." He and Lowell Mason had arranged for a group of boys to demonstrate the effectiveness of music instruction by singing three songs: "The Morning Call," "The Garden," and "The Rising Sun." Wood-

---

1. The moral aspect was the most important.

bridge was a persuasive speaker, and his enthusiasm for music was apparent to his audience. He was a highly respected geographer by profession and a minister, and he was deeply interested in developing the common schools. While in Europe, Woodbridge studied instructional methods. During his second trip to Europe, he observed Nägeli as he applied Pestalozzi's principles. The principles, modified for music instruction, were:

1. To teach sounds before signs—to make the child sing before he learns written notes or their names.
2. To lead the child to observe, by hearing and imitating sounds, their resemblances and differences, their agreeable and disagreeable effects, rather than explaining these things to him. By this principle, the child was to be an active, rather than passive, learner.
3. To teach but one thing at a time—rhythm, melody, expression are taught and practiced separately before the child is called to the difficult task of attending to all at once.
4. To make children practice each step of each of these divisions, until they master it, before passing to the next.
5. To give the principles and theory after practice, and as an induction from it.
6. To analyze and practice the elements of articulate sound in order to apply them to music.
7. To have the names of the notes correspond to those used in instrumental music (Mason 1843, 25–28).

Woodbridge was impressed with what he observed and with the corroborating opinions of Swiss and German educators. He was convinced that music should have a place in the American school curriculum, and that Pestalozzi's approach was superior to that of American singing masters. Upon returning to Connecticut, he joined forces with Elam Ives Jr., an American music teacher who experimented with Pestalozzian principles in teaching music to Hartford children.

Elam Ives Jr. (1802–1864) was born in Hamden, Connecticut. He was a church choir director and singing school master. In 1830, he and his family left Hartford for Philadelphia, where he established the Philadelphia Music Seminary and served as its principal. His pupils gave a concert in Constitution Hall in New York on May 27, 1830. Ives announced during the concert that he planned to establish a new musical seminary in New York, and on September 1, he presented a concert by his New York pupils. He remained in New York almost until the end of his life. Ives later returned to Hamden, where he died in 1864. He wrote many books and art songs from 1830 to 1860 but is virtually forgotten in American music history. He had great impact on music education, and his work as a teacher is historically significant.

Ives was the first to apply Pestalozzian principles to music teaching in the United States. In 1830, he and Woodbridge translated some European materials, which Ives used to teach a volunteer class of about seventy children, ages six to twelve. This was known as the Hartford Experiment. Woodbridge reported that the children were "trained in a few months to sing in a manner which surprised and delighted all who heard them." Ives, pleased with the experiment, prepared two books that demonstrated Pestalozzian principles. A few months later, he had completed the manuscript of his *American Elementary Singing Book*. It may have been the first American music book to advocate Pestalozzian principles (John 1960, 47). His second book, *The Juvenile Lyre*, was published in 1831.

Lowell Mason (1792–1872), the "father of singing among the children" in the United States, was the central figure in the process of having music adopted as a school subject. Mason was born to a prosperous family in Medfield, Massachusetts. His grandfather was a singing school teacher and a schoolmaster. His father owned a dry goods business, was town treasurer, and a member of the state legislature who sang in his church choir and played several instruments. Lowell attended the singing school of Amos Albee and later studied music with Oliver Shaw, a Dedham musician. He played the organ, piano, flute, clarinet, and other instruments.

In 1812, Mason traveled to Savannah, Georgia. No one knows why he went there, but the city might have attracted him because it "must have seemed tropical and remote" (Keating 1989, 74). He worked in a variety store and became a partner after four years. Mason began offering singing schools like those he had directed earlier for church choir members in Massachusetts. In 1815, he became organist and choirmaster of the Independent Presbyterian Church, where he began to compose anthems and hymns. In that same year he helped organize an interdenominational Sabbath school and became its first superintendent. His organizational ability earned him the position of secretary of several organizations, including the Savannah Fencibles (his militia unit), the Savannah Missionary Society, the Sabbath School Teachers Association, the Georgia Bible Society, the Savannah Religious Tract Society, and the Union Society. He also worked in a dry goods store and was town librarian, which required his service three evenings a week. In 1820, he became a clerk in the Planter's Bank, where he worked until he returned to Boston in 1827 (Pemberton 1985, 15).

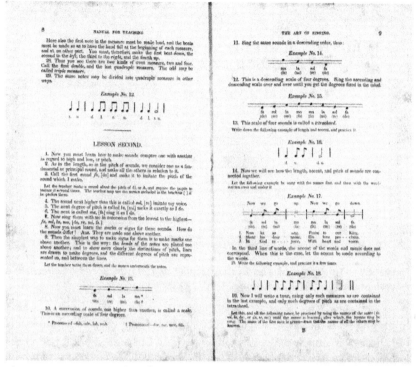

Figure 2.1. Pages 8 and 9 of E. Ives, *A Manual of Instruction in the Art of Singing* (Philadelphia: American Sunday School Union, 1831).

Mason enjoyed a rich musical life in Savannah. He studied harmony and counterpoint with Frederick Abet, a recent immigrant from Germany. His instruction included translating master choruses into English and realizing the figured bass. He also organized concerts advertised as "Grand Oratorios" that featured choruses by Handel, Haydn, and Mozart, as well as solos, duets, hymns, and anthems. Mason was producer, director, performer, program note writer, advertiser, and ticket seller.

Mason compiled his first collection of sacred music while in Savannah. *The Boston Handel and Haydn Society Collection of Church Music* contained some of his own compositions in addition to melodies from instrumental works of Handel, Mozart, and Beethoven. They were adapted for singing by setting the words of familiar hymns and arranged for three and four voices with figured bass for organ or piano. When he completed the collection in 1820, Mason unsuccessfully sought a publisher in Philadelphia and other cities. His fortunes improved when he met Dr. George K. Jackson, organist of the Handel and Haydn Society of Boston. Jackson was

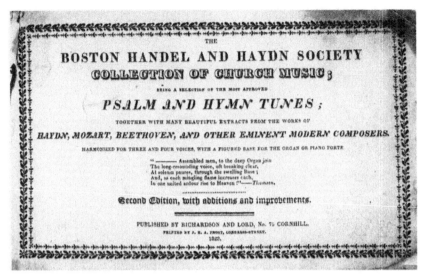

THE

BOSTON HANDEL AND HAYDN SOCIETY
COLLECTION OF CHURCH MUSIC;

BEING A SELECTION OF THE MOST APPROVED

PSALM AND HYMN TUNES ;

TOGETHER WITH MANY BEAUTIFUL EXTRACTS FROM THE WORKS OF

HAYDN, MOZART, BEETHOVEN, AND OTHER EMINENT MODERN COMPOSERS.

HARMONIZED FOR THREE AND FOUR VOICES, WITH A FIGURED BASE FOR THE ORGAN OR PIANO FORTE

" ———— Assembled men, to the deep Organ join
The long-resounding voice, oft breaking clear,
At solemn pauses, through the swelling Base ;
And, as each mingling flame increases each,
In one united ardour rise to Heaven !"———— *Thomson.*

Second Edition, with additions and improvements.

PUBLISHED BY RICHARDSON AND LORD, No. 75 CORNHILL.

PRINTED BY J. H. A. FROST, CONGRESS-STREET.

1823.

Figure 2.2. Title page of *The Boston Handel and Haydn Society Collection of Church Music* **(Boston: Richardson & Lord, 1823).**

impressed with the collection and recommended that the society publish it. He said it was "much the best book of the kind I have seen published in this country." *The Boston Handel and Haydn Society Collection of Church Music* was printed in 1821 and copyrighted in 1822. Mason's name appeared in the preface but he was not identified as the editor. He explained years later, "I was then a bank officer in Savannah and did not wish to be known as a musical man, and I had not the least thought of making music my profession" (Pemberton 1985, 15). The collection went through twenty-two editions, and both Mason and the Handel and Haydn Society earned impressive profits from it. The income was far beyond Mason's expectations. When it brought financial stability and security to the society, he reconsidered becoming a professional musician.

Mason returned to Savannah but came back to Boston in 1826 to lecture on church music. In 1827 he accepted the position of choirmaster of Dr. Lyman Beecher's[2] church. He became president of the Handel and Haydn Society in 1827 but resigned in 1832 to allow more time for teaching children. Mason continued his work as a church musician, and on July 4, 1832, he directed the junior choir of the historic Park Street Church in Boston in the premiere performance of his friend Samuel Francis Smith's "America."

---

2. Lyman Beecher was Harriet Beecher Stowe's father.

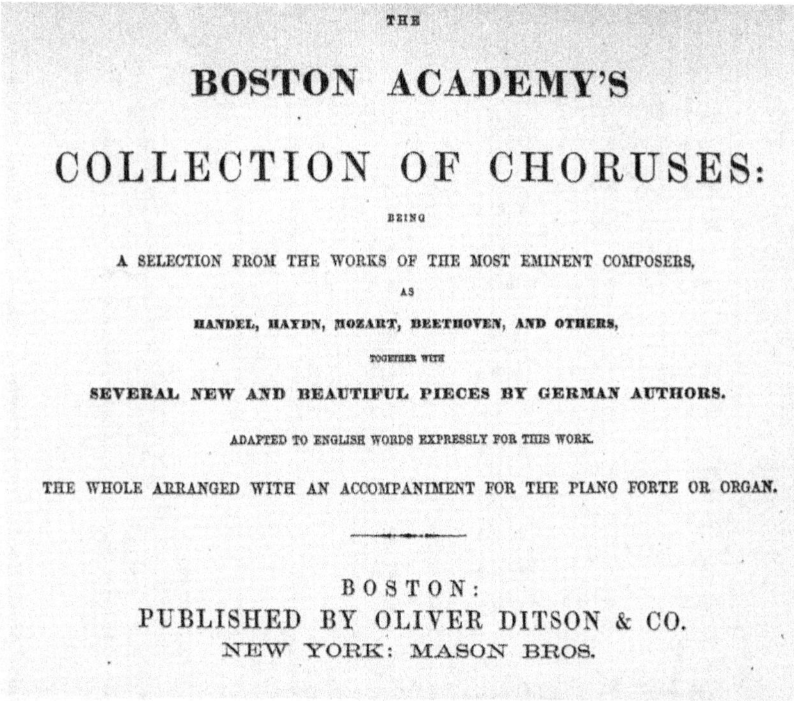

THE

BOSTON ACADEMY'S

COLLECTION OF CHORUSES:

BEING

A SELECTION FROM THE WORKS OF THE MOST EMINENT COMPOSERS,

AS

HANDEL, HAYDN, MOZART, BEETHOVEN, AND OTHERS,

TOGETHER WITH

SEVERAL NEW AND BEAUTIFUL PIECES BY GERMAN AUTHORS.

ADAPTED TO ENGLISH WORDS EXPRESSLY FOR THIS WORK.

THE WHOLE ARRANGED WITH AN ACCOMPANIMENT FOR THE PIANO FORTE OR ORGAN.

BOSTON:

PUBLISHED BY OLIVER DITSON & CO.

NEW YORK: MASON BROS.

Figure 2.3. Title page of *The Boston Academy's Collection of Choruses* (Boston: Oliver Ditson & Co., 1836).

Mason began to publish children's music in 1829. *The Juvenile Psalmist, or The Child's Introduction to Sacred Music*, came out in 1829, and *The Juvenile Lyre* in 1831. He became deeply involved in school music, a part of his career so significant that it will be described separately. Mason founded the Boston Academy of Music in 1832 with George J. Webb and other Boston musicians. Their purpose was to apply Pestalozzian principles in teaching music to children.

Mason and the Nineteenth Century Age of Progress

The eighteenth century Enlightenment, or Age of Reason, gave way to the Age of Progress in nineteenth century America. The word "science" became synonymous with "progress," meaning the new, as opposed to the old-fashioned or archaic. In music, "science" meant disapproval of psalmody in favor of the style of music being composed by European composers of the time like Robert Schumann and Frederic Chopin. Both Schubert and Beethoven had died only a few years earlier. Lowell Mason

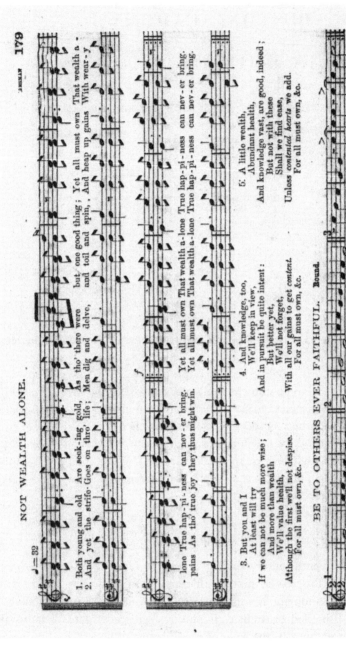

Figure 2.4. Lowell Mason, *The Song Garden: A Series of School Music Books Progressively Arranged, Each Book Complete in Itself,* 2nd book (Boston: Oliver Ditson & Co., 1864).

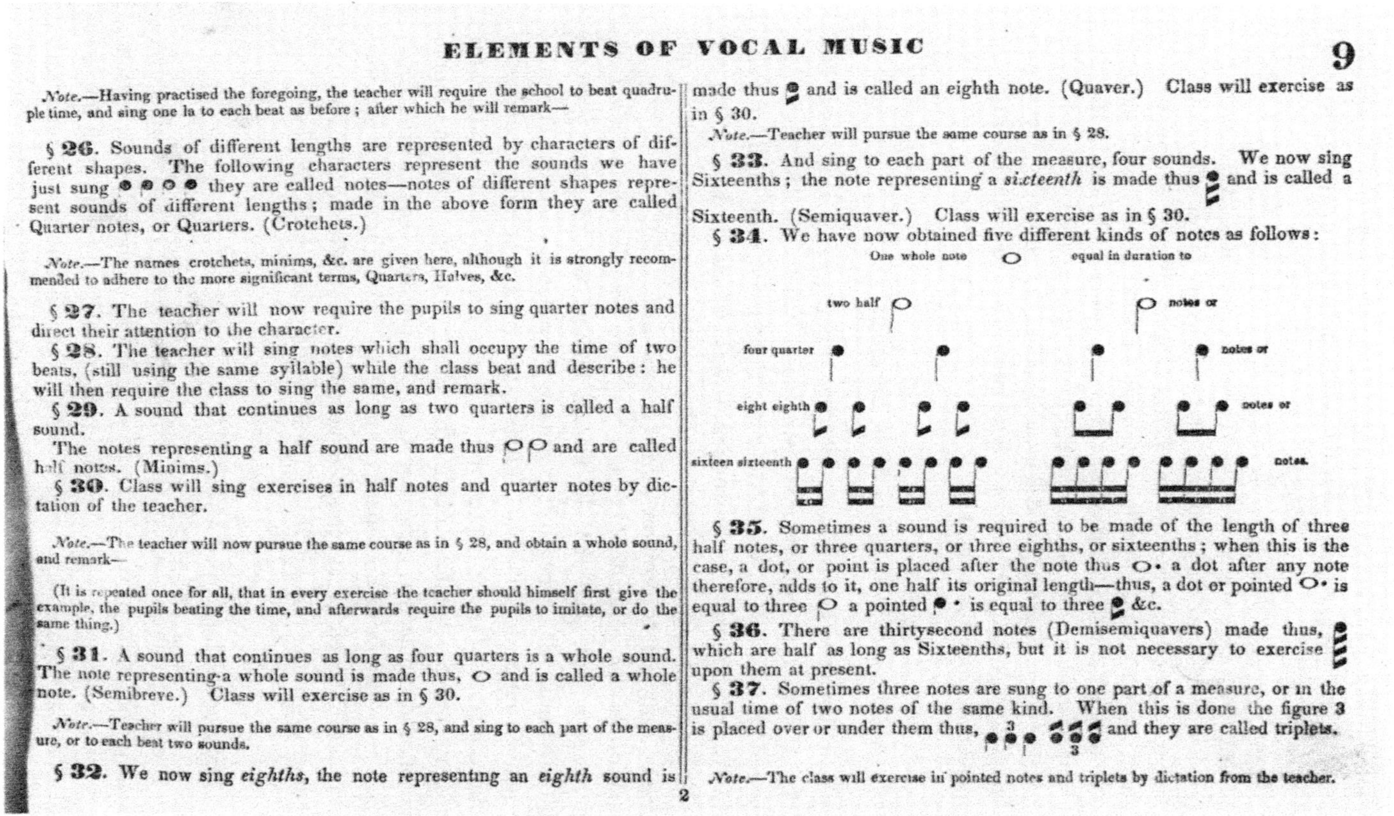

§ 26. Sounds of different lengths are represented by characters of different shapes. The following characters represent the sounds we have just sung ● ● ○ ● they are called notes—notes of different shapes; made in the above form they are called Quarter notes, or Quarters. (Crotchets.)

Note.—The names crotchets, minims, &c. are given here, although it is strongly recommended to adhere to the more significant terms, Quarters, Halves, &c.

§ 27. The teacher will now require the pupils to sing quarter notes and direct their attention to the character.

§ 28. The teacher will sing notes which shall occupy the time of two beats, (still using the same syllable) while the class beat and describe: he will then require the class to sing the same, and remark.

§ 29. A sound that continues as long as two quarters is called a half sound.

The notes representing a half sound are made thus ○○ and are called half notes. (Minims.)

§ 30. Class will sing exercises in half notes and quarter notes by dictation of the teacher.

Note.—The teacher will now pursue the same course as in § 28, and obtain a whole sound, and remark—

(It is repeated once for all, that in every exercise the teacher should himself first give the example, the pupils beating the time, and afterwards require the pupils to imitate, or do the same thing.)

§ 31. A sound that continues as long as four quarters is a whole sound. The note representing a whole sound is made thus, ○ and is called a whole note. (Semibreve.) Class will exercise as in § 30.

Note.—Teacher will pursue the same course as in § 28, and sing to each part of the measure, or to each beat two sounds.

§ 32. We now sing eighths, the note representing an eighth sound is made thus ● and is called an eighth note. (Quaver.) Class will exercise as in § 30.

Note.—Teacher will pursue the same course as in § 28.

§ 33. And sing to each part of the measure, four sounds. We now sing Sixteenths; the note representing a sixteenth is made thus ● and is called a Sixteenth. (Semiquaver.) Class will exercise as in § 30.

§ 34. We have now obtained five different kinds of notes as follows:

One whole note	○	equal in duration to
two half notes		notes or
four quarter notes		notes or
eight eighth notes		notes or
sixteen sixteenth notes		notes.

§ 35. Sometimes a sound is required to be made of the length of three half notes, or three quarters, or three eighths, or sixteenths; when this is the case, a dot, or point is placed after the note thus ○• a dot after any note therefore, adds to it, one half its original length—thus, a dot or pointed ○• is equal to three ○ a pointed ●• is equal to three ● &c.

§ 36. There are thirtysecond notes (Demisemiquavers) made thus, which are half as long as Sixteenths, but it is not necessary to exercise upon them at present.

§ 37. Sometimes three notes are sung to one part of a measure, or in the usual time of two notes of the same kind. When this is done the figure 3 is placed over or under them thus, and they are called triplets.

Note.—The class will exercise in pointed notes and triplets by dictation from the teacher.

Figure 2.5. Page 9 of Luther Whiting Mason, *National Music Course: The New Third Music Reader* (Boston: Ginn & Company, 1888).

promoted this progressive attitude; *The Boston Handel and Haydn Collection of Church Music* was a case in point. He wrote in introduction to the tenth edition (1831):

> Is it to be supposed that in psalmody, science and taste have accomplished all that they can accomplish? and is it desirable that all attempts at improvement should be checked? This is impracticable if it were desirable. . . . Unless, therefore, it be maintained that the present psalm and hymn tunes cannot be improved, and that no better can be substituted in their stead, or else, that bad tunes are as valuable as good ones, there may be as valid reasons, founded in public utility, for introducing alterations into text books of psalmody, as for introducing alterations into text books on arithmetic or grammar.

Pestalozzianism in American Music Education

Woodbridge's impassioned speeches influenced Mason and Ives deeply. Woodbridge collaborated with Mason in August 1830 when he presented his speech "On Vocal Music as a Branch of Common Education" to the American Institute of Instruction. It was his best-known lecture, one that he presented to many audiences. This was the beginning of a long and energetic campaign to promote public school music.

Woodbridge persuaded Ives and Mason to compile *The Juvenile Lyre,* which was published in 1831 by Carter, Hendee & Company (Boston). With this book, Mason began to mature as a teacher of children. The preface stated a rationale for music instruction so persuasive that it supported the introduction of music education in schools throughout the country for almost a century—Pestalozzi's belief that music develops children's moral, physical, and intellectual capacities. Carol Pemberton refers to the *Lyre's* preface as a "landmark document of the early 1830s" because it provided the rationale needed by laypersons to accept music in the schools. For music educators of the time, it was a manifesto (Pemberton 1990, 17–32).

The Boston Academy of Music

The Academy was incorporated in March 1833. One of its objectives was the introduction of "vocal music into schools, by the aid of such teachers as the Academy may be able to employ, each of whom shall instruct classes alternately in a number of schools." Four individuals assumed leadership roles. George H. Snelling, a member of the Boston Primary School Board, responded to Woodbridge's influence and wrote a report recommending that systematic vocal instruction be introduced on an experimental basis in one school in each district (Wilson 1973, 29). The Boston School Committee accepted the report, but then did nothing with it. T. Kemper Davis, an attorney who signed an 1836 petition of twenty-four citizens to include music in the schools, was chairman of a subcommittee on music. Samuel A. Eliot was president of the academy from 1835 to 1847 and was mayor of Boston during the time that negotiations were being carried out with the Boston School Committee (1837–1838). Lowell Mason himself was the fourth figure.

The Boston Academy of Music immediately attracted so many students that it was necessary to hire an additional assistant professor, George J. Webb. The Academy operated vocal music programs in private schools, sponsored public lectures on music, offered music classes to children and adults, worked for the general improvement of church music, and labored to create support for music in the common schools. Professors from the Academy taught music at the Asylum for the Blind, later named the Perkins Institute[3] (Pemberton 1990, 69–70). Eventually, the Academy had a large choir, its own orchestra to accompany oratorios, and by the 1840s it gave performances of symphonic music. It sponsored the translation of Fetis's *Music Explained to the World; or, How to Understand Music and Enjoy its Performance*, which might have been the first attempt at music appreciation in the United States. The Academy was also a demonstration school that highlighted the effectiveness of music instruction.

The Manual of the Boston Academy of Music

In 1834, Lowell Mason published his *Manual of Instruction of the Boston Academy of Music, for Instruction in the Elements of Vocal Music on the System of Pestalozzi*, which became the handbook of singing school teachers throughout the country. The *Manual* guided teachers in teaching music reading through drill with syllables. Mason, not the least bit humble, called himself the "father of singing" among children in this country.

The Music Conventions

Numerous singing societies existed at that time. Small town singing societies often joined with others to perform large choral works and for

---

3. This might have been the first time in the United States that music education served special education students.

contests. In 1829, Henry E. Moore led a singing school convention with the New Hampshire Central Musical Society of Goffstown as a nucleus. The convention was held in September 1829 for two days in Concord, New Hampshire. It attracted church choir directors, singing school masters, and singers from other societies in the region. Similar meetings were held in Pembroke in 1830 and Goffstown in 1831. Mason took it upon himself to establish the Academy as the center of the new convention movement and himself as leader. His *Manual of the Boston Academy of Music* was adopted as the text by most singing school masters.

In August 1834, Mason and George Webb held a convention for eleven men and one woman from Massachusetts, Connecticut, and New Hampshire. There were lectures on teaching methods; classes in psalmody, harmony, and voice culture; and discussions of problems. There was choral practice in the evenings and a concert concluded the convention. The next summer, what Mason called the "class-convention" drew even more students from a larger area. By 1836, the meeting consisted of ten days of lectures on teaching methods, discussion about music education, and church music. The students unanimously approved ten resolutions at the conclusion of the 1836 class-convention:

1. RESOLVED, That the introduction and application of the Pestalozzian System of teaching music form a new era in the science of music education in this country; and, that in pursuing our labors as teachers, we will conform ourselves as far as circumstances will admit, to that system, as published in the *Manual of the Boston Academy of Music.*
2. RESOLVED, That, in order to diffuse a knowledge of music through the community, it is necessary to teach it to our youth; and that it is desirable, and practicable, to introduce it into all our schools, as a branch of elementary education.
3. RESOLVED, That it is the special duty of the Christian Church to cultivate, and encourage the cultivation of Sacred Music generally, as a powerful auxiliary to devotion.
4. RESOLVED, That it is a source of deep regret to this Convention, that, in so many instances, Religious Societies and Parishes, instead of exerting a fostering care and influence over the cause of Sacred Music, neglect it, suffer it to fall into unskillful hands, and thus, not only wound the cause itself, but make it a detriment, rather than a help, to the best interests of the church.

5. RESOLVED, That Singer Choirs too infrequently, in conducting their part of divine worship, attempt the performance of music too difficult, and with which they are not sufficiently familiar, thereby detracting from the solemnity and devotion of the exercise.

6. RESOLVED, That in pursuing our labors as Teachers and Choristers, we will strive to avoid as far as in us lies, any thing like invidious rivalry; and that we will assist each other in our profession as we have opportunity.

7. RESOLVED, That, notwithstanding we have to contend with the prejudice of some, the opposition of others, and the indifference of many, yet we find in the progress of musical education for a few years past, abundant encouragement to persevere in our labors, and not become weary in well-doing.

8. RESOLVED, That the sentiment which prevails in some places, that to occupy a place in the Choir, is not respectable, and, therefore, to assist in one of the most delightful services of the house of God, is not an honorable and dignified employment, is a sentiment founded in ignorance and prejudice; and that those who cherish such a sentiment themselves, or give countenance to it in any way, are endeavoring to subvert an ordinance which God himself has established.

9. RESOLVED, That, in the opinion of this Convention, a good moral character is an Indispensable qualification for a Teacher of Sacred Music, or for a Chorister.

The tenth resolution expressed thanks to Professors Mason and Webb for their "Earnest endeavors and unremitted exertions to qualify us as teachers of vocal music."

The 1838 convention was called the American Musical Convention. It attracted both teachers interested in the methods classes and those who wanted more emphasis on the convention itself. Within a few years, this dichotomy led to disagreements and political intrigue. George Webb severed his connection with the Boston Academy of Music and started his own classes in competition with Mason's. The differences were eventually resolved, and the American Musical Convention continued to train musicians for school and church positions.

The 1840 Academy convention was named The National Music Convention. The conventions grew and spread just as the earlier singing schools had. They attracted skilled musical leaders, either trained by Mason or influenced by him. Mason took his conventions on the road during the 1840s. They were held as far west as Cleveland, but his favorite location was Rochester, New York. Birge wrote: "The Music Convention became our first national school of music pedagogy, harmony, conducting and voice culture" (Birge 1928, 28–29). C. M. Cady of Chicago wrote in a letter to his friend H. S. Perkins:

> For 30 years I have watched the effects of these gatherings upon cities, counties and states in which they have been held under such men as Hastings, Mason, Woodbury, Root and a host of younger conductors. Without exception, so far as my observation has extended, they have resulted in good in many ways, prominent among which are the following:
>
> 1. They have inspired participants with enthusiasm for musical improvement, whether as individuals, choirs, or congregations, and buried petty jealousies under lofty aims.
> 2. They have not only led to better voice culture, better choirs and heartier congregational singing, but have been powerful agents in the introduction of sight-singing into the public schools.
> 3. They have familiarized the public with grand choral effects and the works of the great masters, and to that extent shown the superiority of the sublime over the merely pretty and beautiful. (Birge 1928, 29–30)

The Normal Institutes

Music conventions were held for about thirty years. Students who were primarily interested in teaching wanted the convention to emphasize pedagogy. The others wanted more choral practice. Root suggested a three-month normal institute to be held in New York for those more interested in teaching. The institutes of the 1850s drew students from all over the country and were enormously successful. They offered courses in methods, theory, voice, and piano, taught by William Mason, William H. Sherwood, Frederick W. Root, W. S. B. Mathews, Julia Ettie Crane, Luther Emerson, William W. Killip, Theodore F. Seward, Charles C. Perkins, and George B. Loomis, all outstanding teachers. Mason continued with the institutes until 1862, when he was seventy. The institutes were held in the summer, and some eventually developed into conservatories of music (Birge 1928, 28–29). The other aspect of music conventions, choral singing, also developed separately into choral organizations.

THE BEGINNINGS OF MUSIC IN AMERICAN SCHOOLS

The decade from 1830 to 1840 was especially significant in the establishment of vocal music programs in American schools. Music teachers tried many ways to introduce music into the schools. Some taught for free and others solicited the support of church officials. They secured the cooperation of city officials and the leaders of the common school movement. After vocal music became a curricular subject in Boston schools, citizens throughout the country began to advocate in their communities for music in their own schools. In 1835, the Boston Academy of Music received letters from Georgia, South Carolina, Virginia, Illinois, Missouri, Tennessee, Ohio, Maryland, New York, Connecticut, Vermont, New Hampshire, Maine, and Massachusetts asking how to introduce music in schools (Elson 1915, 35).

Music Becomes a Curricular Subject in Boston

In 1836, Boston citizens submitted two petitions to the Boston School Committee, asking that vocal music be introduced into the school curriculum. The Boston Academy of Music also submitted a request. The School Committee appointed T. Kemper Davis chairman of a new committee on music, charged with making recommendations on the petitions. The special committee examined the work of the Boston Academy of Music and it sent a questionnaire to the principals of five private schools that already offered music as a curricular subject. On August 24, 1837, the Davis committee recommended that vocal music be introduced on an experimental basis in four public schools under the supervision of the Boston Academy of Music. The Davis committee recommendations were published in a lengthy report that revealed the depth of the committee's investigation. The committee made a positive recommendation on the basis of three utilitarian reasons—intellectual, moral, and physical—that mirrored Pestalozzi's legacy. The report stated:

> There is a threefold standard, a sort of chemical test, by which education itself and every branch of education may be tried. Is it intellectual—is it moral—is it physical? Let vocal Music be examined by this standard.
>
> Try it *intellectually*. Music is an intellectual art. Among the seven liberal arts, which scholastic ages regarded as pertaining to humanity, Music had its place. Arithmetic, Geometry, Astronomy and Music, these formed the *quadrivium*. Separate degrees in Music, it is believed, are still conferred by the University of Oxford. Memory, comparison,

attention, intellectual faculties all of them, are quickened by the study of its principles. It is not ornamental only. It has high intellectual affinities. It may be made, to some extent, an intellectual discipline.

Try music *morally*. There is—who has not felt it—a mysterious connection, ordained undoubtedly for wise purposes, between certain sounds and the moral sentiments of man. This is not to be gainsaid, neither is it to be explained. It is an ultimate law of man's nature. "In Music," says Hooker, "the very image of virtue and vice is perceived." Now it is a curious fact, that the natural scale of musical sound can only produce good, virtuous, and kindly feelings. You must reverse this scale, if you would call forth the sentiments of a corrupt, degraded, and degenerate character. Has not the finger of the Almighty written here an indication too plain to be mistaken? And if such be the case, if there be this necessary concordance between certain sounds and certain trains of moral feeling, is it unphilosophical to say that exercises in vocal Music may be so directed and arranged as to produce those habits of feeling of which these sounds are types. Besides, happiness, contentment, cheerfulness, tranquility—these are the natural effects of Music. These qualities are connected intimately with the moral government of the individual. Why should they not, under proper management, be rendered equally efficient in the moral government of the school?

And now try music *physically*. "A fact," says an American physician, "has been suggested to me by my profession, which is, that the exercise of the organs of the breast by singing contributes very much to defend them from those diseases to which the climate and other causes expose them." A musical writer in England after quoting this remark, says, the "Music Master of our Academy has furnished me with an observation still more in favor of this opinion. He informs me that he had known several persons strongly disposed to consumption restored to health, by the exercise of the lungs in singing." But why cite medical or other authorities to a point so plain? It appears self-evident that exercise in vocal Music, when not carried to an unreasonable excess, must expand the chest, and thereby strengthen the lungs and vital organs.

Judged, then by this triple standard, intellectually, morally, and physically, vocal Music seems to have a natural place in every system of instruction which aspires, as should every system, to develope [*sic*] man's whole nature. (School Committee 1837, 123)

The most significant resolutions were the following:

RESOLVED, That in the opinion of the School Committee, it is expedient to try the experiment of introducing vocal Music, by Public authority, as part of the system of Public Instruction, into the Public schools of this City.

RESOLVED, That the experiment be tried in the four following schools, the Hancock school, for Girls, in Hanover street; the Eliot school, for Boys, in North Bennett street; the Johnson school, for Girls, in Washington street; and the Hawes school, for Boys and Girls, at South Boston.

RESOLVED, That this experiment be given in charge to the Boston Academy of Music, under the direction of the Board, and that a Committee of five be appointed from the Board to confer with the Academy, arrange all necessary details of the plan, oversee its operation, and make quarterly report thereof to the Board. (School Committee 1836, 138)

The Boston School Committee approved the report on September 19, 1837, but the Boston Common Council refused to appropriate funds. Mason was determined. He offered to teach for one year at the Hawes School in South Boston with no salary. The School Committee agreed to his proposal on November 14, 1837. The final agreement contained several compromises: only one school, rather than four, would receive music instruction; there would be no public funding; and significantly, the experiment was controlled by the Boston School Committee rather than by the Boston Academy of Music (Wilson 1973, 110–31).

Mason taught at the Hawes School during the 1837–1838 school year. Mayor Samuel Eliot was pleased by a report from the school that year:

Many who at the outset of the experiment believed they had neither ear or voice, now sing with confidence and considerable accuracy; and others who could hardly tell one sound from another, now sing the scale with ease; sufficiently proving that the musical susceptibility is in a good degree improvable. The alacrity with which the lesson is entered upon, and the universal attention with which it is received, are among its great recommendations; they show that the children are agreeably employed; and we are certain that they are innocently employed. We have never known, when, unless extraordinary engagements prevented, they were so glad to remain a half-hour or more, to pursue the exercise after the regular hours of session. They prefer the play of a hard musical lesson to any out-of-door sports; of course understanding that there are some exceptions. Of the great moral effect of vocal music, there can be no question. A song introduced in the middle of the session, has been invariably followed with excellent effect. It is a relief to the wearisomeness of constant study. It excites the listless, and calms the turbulent and uneasy. It seems to renerve [*sic*] the mind, and prepare all for more vigorous intellectual action. (Boston Musical Gazette 1838)

The annual school exhibition was held on August 14 in the South Baptist Church. It began with the song "Flowers, Wild Wood Flowers" (Birge 1928, 53).

The Magna Charta of Music Education

The concert convinced many people that music should be included in the curriculum, and on August 28, 1838, the Boston School Committee approved a motion to allow the Committee on Music to employ a teacher of vocal music in the public schools of Boston. Music was approved for the first time in the United States as a subject of the public school curriculum, equal to other subjects, and supported with school funds. Music had been taught in schools before, but never as an integral curricular subject. This landmark action was referred to in the annual report of the Boston Academy of Music (July 1, 1839) as the "Magna Charta of Music Education" (Birge, 55).

Mason was appointed Superintendent of Music, the first supervisor of music in the United States. He hired Jonathan Woodman, organist of the Boston Academy, to assist him. In the second year, he hired A. N. Johnson, G. F. Root, A. J. Drake, and J. A. Johnson to teach music in the Boston grammar schools and in two suburbs. By 1844, Mason was teaching in six schools and supervising ten teachers in ten more schools.

There was a negative side to Mason's success, however. Some of the Boston music teachers were jealous of his achievements. H. W. Day, a Boston tune-book compiler, singing school master, and editor of the *American Journal of Music and Musical Visitor*, criticized Mason publicly. Day accused Mason, a Congregationalist, of hiring only Congregationalists to teach in the schools. He pointed out that Benjamin Baker, the only teacher who was not a Congregationalist, had been fired in 1845. Activist Unitarians protested Baker's firing. Day also said that Mason earned too much money for his position. He received $130 a year for each school with a music program. The teacher was paid $80, $20 was spent for piano rental, and Mason kept the remaining $30. Day also attacked Mason's teaching, saying that he (Mason) did not really understand Pestalozzianism and that his students did not learn enough (Flueckiger 1936, 20–21). Day's letter-writing campaign and newspaper articles convinced the Boston School Committee that Mason had to be replaced:

> Day had escalated a previous state of professional animosity among musicians into a continual and public state of siege upon Mason. The

School Committee was without doubt embarrassed by Day's editorializing, which, in effect, made members out to be goats for allowing Mason to work the schools for personal financial gain and aggrandizement at the expense of the city.

The committee did not accuse Mason of impropriety or incompetence but nevertheless voted to fire him with no opportunity to defend himself. Mason lost his job in 1845 without official warning or recourse (Wilson, 132). He still had strong political support from former school committee members, however, and from Horace Mann and the next mayor of Boston, Josiah Quincy Jr. Mason was rehired six months later and remained in the Boston public schools until 1851 (Wilson, 132).

School Music Spreads to Other Communities

Cincinnati, Ohio, was a leader among other American cities in establishing school music programs. Its history is similar to Boston's. The majority of Cincinnati's early citizens were from New York, New Jersey, and Pennsylvania, but its community leaders were from New England. Many were graduates of Harvard, Yale, and Dartmouth. Many eminent men came to the city to join the faculties of a medical school and a theological seminary. Nathaniel D. Gould, a music historian, wrote: "Cincinnati, sometimes called the Queen City, seems to stand in the same musical relation to the western country as Boston does to the eastern, that is, the musical and other educational institutions of the respective regions centre in those cities" (Gould 1853, 138).

A year after the Boston Academy of Music was founded, Cincinnatians formed the Eclectic Academy of Music "to aid in promoting the introduction of vocal music as a branch of education throughout this country" (*Cincinnati Daily Gazette* 1834, 2). Timothy Mason, Lowell's brother, came from Boston to accept the position of professor. The esteemed preacher Lyman Beecher had just come west to head the new Lane Seminary and to be the pastor of the Second Presbyterian Church. He had left Bowdoin Street Church in Boston and Lowell Mason's outstanding choir, and was anxious for Timothy Mason to create a new choir in Cincinnati (Gould 1853, 138).

Cincinnati had a strong cultural base. The Western Literary Institute and College of Professional Teachers of Cincinnati met each October to hear papers on education. In 1834, William Nixon was the first to advocate for music education in Cincinnati. He and his wife established the Logerian

Musical Institute[4] on Fourth Street. Calvin E. Stowe read an important paper at the Institute's Seventh Annual Meeting in 1837. He had recently returned from Europe with his wife, the former Harriet Beecher. They had visited schools and were especially impressed with the teaching of music in Prussia. Stowe's address was entitled the "Course of Instruction in the Schools of Prussia and Wurtemberg." He said:

> This branch of instruction can be introduced into all our common schools with the greatest advantage, not only to the comfort and discipline of the pupils, but also to their progress in their other studies. . . . The students are taught from the blackboard. The different sounds are represented by lines of different lengths, by letters, and by musical notes; and the pupils are thoroughly drilled on each successive principle before proceeding to the next. (Stowe 1838, 217)

Stowe later presented his report before the Ohio legislature, where it became one of the most discussed education documents of its time.

Timothy Mason and Harriet Stowe's brother, Charles Beecher, presented another critically important paper at the 1837 meeting. They drew three conclusions: "(1) All men can learn to sing; (2) Vocal music is of physical, intellectual, and moral benefit as a school subject; and (3) To bring about the introduction of music to the schools the 'public mind must be made ready to recognize its desirability' and the 'teachers must be qualified.'" The report mentioned the Boston Academy Class Conventions: "Twenty-three gentlemen thus instructed have gone into the various parts of the United States and instructed with success. . . . In this city also, we are aware of two teachers of public schools, who have been successful in introducing the study into their schools." They pointed out that there was no reason why every teacher should not be expected "as a part of his profession to teach both vocal and instrumental music." All that was needed, they argued, was for the educators of the country to encourage men of professional talent to "cast themselves hand and heart into the grand work of education." The Institute accepted the report and passed a resolution:

> Resolved, as the settled sentiment of this convention, that the capacity for vocal music is common to mankind, and that vocal music may be employed to great advantage as a means of discipline, of health, and of intellectual and moral advancement; and ought to be part of the daily

---

4. Logerian was a system of singing.

course of instruction, in all our common schools, as well as higher seminaries. (Stowe 1838, 18)

Music was taught formally for the first time in the Cincinnati schools in 1838, possibly by the two men Timothy Mason mentioned in the Mason and Beecher report. Mason himself went into the schools and conducted classes for no salary as his brother had done earlier that year in Boston. When the Logerian Institute convened in October 1838 at the Sixth Street Methodist Church, "several select pieces were sung by a large number of pupils of the Common Schools, led by Mr. Mason" (*Cincinnati Daily Gazette* 1838, 2). The juvenile choir, composed of pupils of several city schools, was featured twice. In June, "volunteer exercises in singing, by a portion of the pupils" was part of the Annual Procession and Exhibition of the Common Schools of Cincinnati (Board of Trustees 1838).

Music was offered for the first time in the Cincinnati common schools in the school year 1837–1838. The annual report of the public schools mentioned music:

> Music has been taught and practised in several of the schools, not by any request of the Board of Trustees, but as a means of rational amusement . . . a useful auxiliary in the promotion of good order. They think it has a tendency to render study more easy and pleasant, to produce a greater harmony of voices and a stronger union of hearts.

Classroom teachers and community volunteers continued to lead classroom singing while the board debated during the next few years whether to hire music instructors. William F. Coburn and Elizabeth Thatcher finally were hired to begin teaching on August 12, 1844 (the Cincinnati schools were on an eleven-month schedule at that time). Coburn's salary of $45 a month for thirteen and a half hours a week in the schools indicates that "music professors" were considered highly qualified because male principals earned the same amount. Thatcher taught one-third as many hours and was paid twelve dollars a month, three dollars less than the lowest paid full-time women teachers.

Charles Aiken joined the staff in 1848 and soon became Cincinnati's most prominent figure in public school music. He was a Dartmouth graduate who worked his way west conducting singing schools. His brother, John Calvin Aiken, attended Lowell Mason's 1836 convention and another brother, Henry, was a soloist with the Boston Handel and Haydn Society. There is no record of Charles Aiken studying with any of the Boston Academy professors. Aiken taught for thirty-one years in Cincinnati and was the first music specialist to teach in the primary grades. He mentored a staff that produced instructional books for use in the Cincinnati schools (*The Young Singer, The Young Singer's Manual, The Cincinnati Music Readers*), and he was the city's first superintendent of music. He compiled two books of choral music for high schools, *The High School Choralist* and *The Choralist's Companion*.

Music Education in Other Cities

Several large cities established music programs before the Civil War (1861–1865), although music did not always remain in the curriculum. Music was a high school subject in San Francisco in 1851, before it was a curricular subject in the grammar schools. Galveston, Texas, began a program in 1847 and San Antonio in 1853. Detroit began a music program in the 1850s. Chicago, Memphis, Saint Louis, Terra Haute, Cleveland, and Columbus had music instruction in their schools. Many cities established programs after the Civil War. An early example of state funding for music, rather than local funding, was the Texas Institute for the Blind in 1857 (Kapfer 1967, 191–200).

The New Music Education Literature

The early school music programs were the genesis of music education as we know it today, but Lowell Mason and his colleagues were criticized many years later for their choice of music. They replaced the indigenous music of the singing school with music typical of the less prominent European composers. Allen Britton wrote:

> By 1838, when Lowell Mason succeeded in introducing music to the public schools, music teachers found to be better music the blander and, to modern ears, more insipid music of English and third-rate Continental composers, and such music was gradually adopted . . . to replace the virile native product of the days of early sovereignty. . . . Since folk or popular music has been considered to lack gentility, and since the highly artistic forms of European art music have been little understood by the public, the music educator has found himself in the position of trying to find understandable music that could be taken as "classical." The term "polite" is perhaps as good as any other to characterize much of the music utilized in schools from the time of Lowell Mason to the present day. (Britton 1961, 214–15)

Britton's view of the quality of music education literature raises the question of why music educators chose to look down on their native music in favor of a bland, innocuous genre with no obvious redeeming characteristics. They used this music because many Americans considered European culture to be more advanced than their own at a time when the United States was still young. English colonists in America had always remained tied to the musical life of the mother country. When English parish church congregations began singing fuging tunes and adding graces and ornaments, Americans did the same. There was a break in the relationship in the second half of the eighteenth century as America sought independence. American singing school masters of that period created their own style. They flourished in isolation from Europe, first during the Revolution and later in the rural southern and western regions of America. European musicians reappeared on the scene when the two countries restored relations. Again, Americans looked to European culture for leadership. But Lowell Mason, Thomas Hastings, and others who wrote for both school and church adopted a style that was neither vigorous nor innovative.

In addition, textbook writers were concerned with children's moral development; taste in music, prose, and poetry was secondary. The *McGuffey Readers* that were used almost universally to teach reading leaned heavily toward moral development, rather than giving children an appetite for literature. Music textbooks paralleled the *McGuffey Readers*. Children's interest in fine music was expected to come later, when they had learned to read and could participate in performances of European oratorios. Nineteenth century music educators believed that children should learn to read music before being introduced to the choruses.

There was another, more crass reason for Mason's choice of music. Mason and his colleagues had excellent business sense. They saw clearly that they could establish a huge demand that only they could fill by creating a need for new music. They were right, and they made a great deal of money in the process. It is interesting to consider what might have been accomplished in American schools if a more musical genre of literature was selected as the foundation for education in music.

Mason was among the first to introduce European-style music into schools. Other books containing that kind of music were also published. *The Child's Song Book, for the Use of Schools and Families, Being a Selection of Favourite Airs, with Hymns and Moral Songs, Suitable for Infant Instruction*[5]

---

5. The phrase "Infant Instruction" referred at that time to young children, probably in the earliest grades in school, and not to babies in their first year as we understand the phrase today.

was published by Richard, Lord & Holbrook (Boston) in 1830. The title of *The Child's Song Book* suggests that hymns and moral songs were sung in schools as early as 1830.

The publisher's introduction to *The Sacred Harp or Eclectic Harmony* offered an explanation of how the works of European classical composers came to be included in American songbooks by compilers like Lowell Mason:

> Subjects or arrangements were included from celebrated composers, as Beethoven, Haydn, Mozart and others. These authors never wrote psalm and hymn tunes. The tunes ascribed to them are themes from their various works, and arranged in their present form by other composers. In many instances, only the principal ideas contained in the tune, have been derived from the author to whom it has been ascribed. In such cases, more or less of the tune is the composition of the arranger, and it is usual to say, "Subject from Beethoven . . . Arranged from Mozart," "Arranged from Gregorian Chant," &c. Many composers have in this way greatly extended the boundaries of Psalmody, and added much to the richness and variety of church music. . . . To arrange psalmody from such peculiar materials with judgment, accuracy, and elegance, as much scientific knowledge and labor are requisite as for composing new tunes.

Music of this type was introduced into this country in the *Handel and Haydn Collection*, by Lowell Mason, and his arrangements from European subjects in that work have often been inserted in other publications *without permission* (Britton 1961, 214–15).

MUSIC EDUCATION IN AN ERA OF INDUSTRIALIZATION

After the Civil War, pragmatic administrators were not interested in music instruction for the sake of enjoyment or beauty. As the nation created an industrial society, school boards and administrators favored subjects that reflected the mechanization of the Industrial Revolution and that would prepare students for their future work. They wanted subjects organized scientifically and evaluated accurately. In 1843, Thomas Lothrop, superintendent of the Buffalo, New York, schools, wrote:

> Musical instruction should be systematized and become a part of the graded course, both teachers and pupils being held to a strict account for the amount of their work in this as other studies, by term and annual

examinations. By a careful apportionment of the elementary principles among the different grades the pupils will secure, while learning the sounds and combinations of letters required in reading the language they speak, such a familiarity with music that they can read it as readily as the letters of the alphabet. (Buttelman 1937, 80)

Music as a almost standardized test

The Music Specialist

The elementary schools were created to teach the elements, and music specialists attempted to do exactly that. The respected English philosopher Herbert Spencer stated that the arts could be taught scientifically; in that milieu, music teachers developed materials and methods that presented information about music in a "scientific" way. Knowledge about music was important, and pupils were tested regularly. Music sight-reading was taught like other subjects with recitation by individual students.

Classroom teachers were directly responsible for teaching the elements of music and for developing skills. Music specialists became supervisors who visited the schools on a regular schedule to supervise the classroom teachers. The specialists tested the pupils, helped improve the quality of their singing, and assigned new material to be learned. This was a common practice that created the title *supervisor* for school music specialists. It was begun in some school systems as early as the 1850s.

Music Instructional Material

Supervisors prepared books, charts, and examinations; they created series of daily drill exercises and prescribed songs. The involvement of classroom teachers influenced the textbooks. The movable *do* had been almost universally adopted by then. School music still meant singing, and much of the song material was created for didactic purposes. Texts were designed to teach secularized lessons drawn from Protestant Christian morality. Supervisors emphasized methodology as school music expanded and it became an important part of textbook publishers' business.

Graded Music Series

The first graded music series appeared in the late 1860s to help children learn to read music. Lowell Mason and his followers believed in the Pestalozzian concept of the "thing before the sign," which later became known as the rote song method. Others believed that children should learn to read printed music before they sang songs. This pedagogical controversy lasted throughout the rest of the nineteenth century. Mason was the first to use the phrase *graded music series* when he described his *The Song Garden*, a three-volume set that he began in 1864.

Joseph Bird published a pamphlet in 1850 entitled *To Teachers of Music*, in which he disagreed with Mason's rote method that he advocated in the *Manual of the Boston Academy of Music*. In his pamphlet, Bird wrote:

> Teach a class by rote and the "Elements" and a few will read, but the greater number give up in despair. . . . We believe the only way by which reading music will become as universal as the reading of our language is by changing the system, and making books and teaching from them in the same way we do from our reading books.

Bird's two-volume set, *Vocal Music Readers*, intended for primary and grammar grades, was published by the Oliver Ditson Company in 1861. Osborne McConathy criticized Bird's method in a letter to the *Louisville Journal*.

> There are two methods adopted by professors of music in teaching children to sing. To illustrate what I mean, it is a uniform habit with some masters of vocal and instrumental music too, to begin as soon as the children have learned the names of the notes, with very little else, to set them to singing by leading off by the sound of his flute or violin or with his voice, and then require the children to give the same sound by imitating his as best they can. This I call mimicry or teaching to sing by imitation, just as the parrot might catch the air and learn to sing, and to sing tunes readily, and yet not understand anything truly valuable concerning the true principles of music. This method of teaching music lays the foundation in error and hedges up the way to a thorough understanding of this branch of ornamental science. . . . The other method of teaching is directly the reverse of the foregoing, and the master endeavors in the first place to teach the children the principles of music whether vocal or instrumental, and to cause the children to understand them well before he allows them to commence singing. . . . Our children should be thoroughly taught the principles of music, and to such a degree of perfection as to enable them to read off a piece of music with as much ease and readiness as they would read a lesson in prose. . . . A child so taught needs no prompter. He needs no one to lead off upon his flute or fiddle. He makes use of his eyes and not his ears only, and practically employs the intellectual instruction imparted and received, and tunes the voice in varied tones and measures of sweetest melody and enrapturing song. (John 1954, 104)

George Loomis

George Loomis, the Indianapolis music supervisor, produced *First Steps in Music* in 1866. This three-volume series introduced music reading by placing notes above or around a single line. Staff lines were gradually added until the pupils were reading from a full staff. The first volume contained exercises and songs on staves of varying numbers of lines. Loomis did not use clefs, meter or key signatures, or accidentals.

The second book contained short songs and rounds on five line staves. It, too, had no clef signs or key signatures, although Loomis indicated the key with a system of his own invention. A number was placed on the staff where the key signature would normally appear. Ivison, Blakeman, Taylor and Company eventually obtained the rights to the series and published it under the title *Progressive Music Lessons*. *The Progressive Glee and Chorus Book* came out in 1879. In 1898, the American Book Company purchased the publication rights. The series was widely used throughout the Midwest during the 1870s and 1880s (John 1954, 110).

In January 1856, Luther Whiting Mason moved from Louisville to join the music staff of the Cincinnati public schools. There, Mason was introduced to the works of Christian Heinrich Hohmann, and he used Hohmann's materials in his teaching from that time on. The charts that he prepared from Hohmann were approved by the Board of Trustees in 1862. With D. H. Baldwin, who later founded the Baldwin Piano Company, Mason was responsible for the "Elements of Music" section of *The Young Singer*, the first of many books prepared by the Cincinnati music staff.

In 1864, Mason relocated to Boston to instruct lower grades with the title Superintendent of Music in the Primary Schools. In the years 1864–1865, H. S. Perkins reported that 14 to 15 percent of the grammar school pupils could not sing, but in 1869, after Luther Whiting Mason had worked in the primary grades for four years, the proportion had been reduced to 7 percent (Perkins 1908, 5–9).

Mason stressed the importance of teaching a body of rote songs while making the elements of music clear to students. He borrowed the use of charts from Hohmann and was responsible for their popularity. Mason began by using the first five notes of the G-major scale, which he taught in a variety of small motives working from one to two measures, to four measures, and finally to eight measures. He employed his own time names and the rests were whispered (Hartley 1960).

The National Music Course

Luther Mason's belief in the value of rote singing as the initial experience for children made him an outstanding figure in American music education. He wrote a pivotal graded series called *The National Music Course*, published in 1870 by Ginn Brothers of Boston (soon to become Ginn and Company). Julius Eichberg, J. B. Sharland, and H. E. Holt were also listed as authors. The series became the accepted text from New England to San Francisco almost immediately. The overwhelming popularity of *The National Music Course* helped Ginn and Company become financially stable as it grew to be a leading publisher of school texts (Hartley 1960). *The National Music Course,* side-bound like most books rather than end-bound in the style of the singing schools, was a model for future graded series.

The National Music Course consisted of seven books: five readers, an intermediate volume that included books two and three, and an abridged fourth reader. It included sets of charts to provide a sequential approach to music reading through all the grades. Much of the song material was based on German folk music (John, 111). The introduction described the philosophy of the authors:

> "Singing as it happens," . . . is that which is most common among the people. It is fostered and vigorously perpetuated in our Sunday Schools, and in common schools where no regular instruction in music is given, and where the object is to have the children sing a few simple melodies, without reference to musical culture as such. . . . This kind of singing is not altogether useless, as in many cases there is a freshness and energy about it which serves to awaken a love for singing, and to furnish a basis on which to build a subsequent course of musical instruction.
>
> But there is a wide distinction between this haphazard singing and genuine "Rote-Singing." The latter is the most important part of instruction, without which in fact there can be no real tuition in vocal music. Genuine rote-singing . . . leads to a discrimination between a musical and unmusical style. . . . We propose in the course of instruction indicated in the series of *National Music Readers and Charts* to do away with all haphazard singing. We therefore, start with a regular course of instruction in rote singing, as indicated in the *National Music Teacher*; and we endeavor to preserve all the freshness and energy of the "singing as it happens" without any of its vicious qualities. (Mason 1870, iii–iv)

Students were expected to learn "all the alphabet of music in a practical way." Rote singing was continued in the second book, but students began to apply their knowledge of notation to learn two part songs after hearing them played only once or twice. They sang the song texts the third time. Mason included detailed, prescriptive lesson plans to guide classroom teachers as they provided most of the music instruction with the assistance of the music supervisors. Lesson I of the *New Second Music Reader* (1888) follows:

> Lesson I
>
> Beating Two-art Measure.—Position.
>
> Teacher. Attention!
>
> [The pupils give their attention.]
>
> T. Place your hands as I do mine!
>
> [a. The teacher places her hands so that the end of the middle finger of the right hand shall rest in the centre of the palm of the left, and draws the elbows well back, bringing the forearms into a horizontal position, quite close to the body. The pupils imitate her with more or less success at first, but finally all do it very well, for it is not very difficult.]
>
> T. You are doing very well indeed. Now watch me, and do as I do!

Figure 2.6. Title page from Luther Whiting Mason, *National Music Teacher: A Practical Guide in Teaching Vocal Music and Sight-Singing to the Youngest Pupils in Schools and Families* (Boston: Ginn Brothers, 1872).

[b. The teacher raises her hand from its horizontal position to a nearly upright one, by a quick motion from the wrist only, and keeps her hand in that position. The pupils imitate her.]

T. [With her hand still in upright position.] When I say, Position for beating time, I wish you to place your hands as you have them now. Watch me again, and do as I do. Attention!

Teacher drops her hands at her sides. The class imitates her.]

T. Very well. Position for beating time!

[Many of the pupils understand, and take the position promptly; some move indolently, others place the left hand above the right, and so on.]

T. Some of you did quite well. But I want you all to do it well; and to do that, you must be smart, quick, about it.

When I say, Attention, drop your hands at your sides. Attention!

[Teacher drops hands at her sides. The pupils imitate her.]

T. Position for beating time!

[Teacher again takes position, as at b, and the pupils imitate her more successfully, as a class, than at first. As this is the first step, it will be better to be quite sure of it before proceeding farther; and it may need several trials to enable all to take the position promptly.]

In Lesson II, the pupils learn to actually beat the two part measure,[6] in Lesson III the three part measure, and in Lesson IV the four part measure. Similar lessons follow for melodic notation, rhythm, and meter.

Mason's books brought him international recognition and respect. The Emperor of Japan invited Mason to introduce his method to Japanese music teachers because he wanted to bring Western culture to his country. Mason taught in Japan for three years with the title Governmental Music Supervisor, teaching what was called *Mason Song* to Japanese music teachers.[7] Later, Mason traveled to Germany, where his work was also highly respected. A letter to his ten-year-old twin grandsons provides an insight to him:

December 8, 1889

Louis and Luther:

It is now getting very near to the first of January, 1890 when I must settle up with you. You must remember that for every day, except Sunday, that you neglect to practice 45 minutes, you lose twenty-five cents;

6. The second lesson only covers the *position* for beating the two part measure.
7. American baseball was introduced to Japan not much later, and both American music education and baseball have been part of Japanese culture since the last part of the nineteenth century.

8

NEW THIRD NATIONAL MUSIC READER.

FIFTHS, PERFECT AND DIMINISHED.

There is the same reason for calling the fifths *perfect*, as there is for the *fourths*, as will appear in our future lessons.

A Perfect Fifth contains three tones and one semitone, as may be seen by looking at the diagram of fifth.

You will also see that all the fifths are perfect except that from the seventh degree of the scale, which is diminished, as it contains two tones and two semitones.

The Diminished Fifth is designated by a small cipher after the Roman numerals which stand for the third, thus: vII₅.

The fifths appear on the staff thus:

Fifths do not sound well when sung consecutively.

"Note that the one imperfect fifth is formed on the 7th of the scale.

"Like the augmented fourth, the imperfect fifth is rather an interval of harmony than of melody, and for precisely the same reason. It is composed of the same characteristic sounds of the scale (the 4th and 7th), which again tend toward the most important sounds of the tonic chord (the 3rd and 8th).

"Form the class in two divisions.

"Sing after me this note.

"First division sing *Do Fa*, and sustain *Fa*; second division sing *Do Si*, and sustain *Si*. Then—

"First division pass from *Fa to Mi*; second division from *Si to Do*."

—HULLAH.

Diagram of Fifths.

9

BOOK 1.—TWO-PART SONG.

EXERCISES IN FIFTHS.

From "Time and Tune," by JOHN HULLAH.

SILCHER.

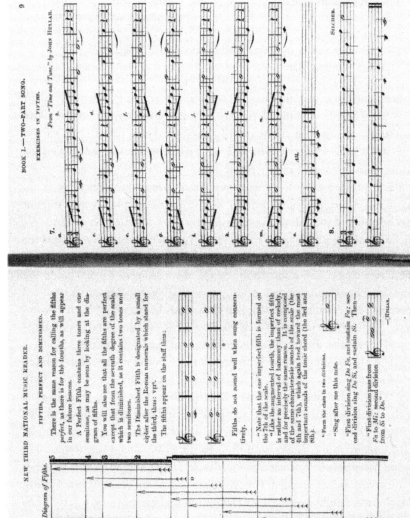

Figure 2.7. Page 9 from Luther Whiting Mason's *New National Music Reader.*

and for every page that you can play to your Mama without making a mistake you gain twenty-five cents.

If this plan works well and you wish to keep it up, I will send your father $100 on the first of January, 1890, so you can go over. I will also allow you twenty-five cents a page for the violin. So your Mama and Papa must examine you and write to me so I can make a settlement with you and begin again. . . .

I shall write you again soon. Your affectionate Grandpa,

Luther Whiting Mason

Daily practice was the key to classroom vocal music lessons. Most schools allotted fifteen minutes in the schedule each day for music. The organization of many of the textbooks supported this pattern. All of the books of *The Model Music Course* had eight chapters, each to be studied for a month, and thirty-two one-week lessons.

Benjamin Jepson's *The Elementary Music Reader* (published by A. S. Barnes) was a serious competitor to Mason's series. Jepson was a singing school master and the son of an oratorio singer. He resigned his commission in the army after losing part of an ear to a Confederate sharpshooter and returned to New Haven, Connecticut, in late 1864. He began teaching music at the Cedar Street School in 1865 (*School Music Monthly* 1903, 11). At the end of the school year, he staged a Public School Music Rehearsal attended by parents, Yale faculty, ministers, citizens, and the mayor of New Haven. The successful event included sight-singing demonstrations and choral singing, and it ensured the future of vocal music in the New Haven schools.

In 1871, Jepson published the first of three books of the series entitled *The Elementary Music Reader*. It consisted of exercises interspersed with songs. The second and third books were published in 1873. Jepson's goal was the achievement of sight-reading skills, and the sight-reading material in the third book was very difficult. In 1888, he wrote a revision of *The Elementary Music Reader* with the new title, *Standard Music Reader*. The *Standard Music Reader* consisted of four books for eight grades. His last series was a six-volume set entitled *The New Standard Music Reader* (New Haven, 1904). Jepson taught in the New Haven schools for more than forty years (John, 112).

The Normal Music Course

By the 1880s, school administrators had become concerned that music was more of an entertainment than an educational experience. School systems throughout the country were adopting music, and administrators

THE

NORMAL MUSIC COURSE

A SERIES OF EXERCISES, STUDIES, AND SONGS, DEFINING AND ILLUSTRATING THE
ART OF SIGHT READING, PROGRESSIVELY ARRANGED FROM THE FIRST
CONCEPTION AND PRODUCTION OF TONES TO THE
MOST ADVANCED CHORAL PRACTICE.

SECOND READER

NEW EDITION. REVISED AND ENLARGED.

BY

JOHN W. TUFTS

AND

H. E. HOLT.

SILVER, BURDETT & CO., Publishers

(Successors to SILVER, ROGERS & CO.),
6 HANCOCK AVENUE, BOSTON.
31 East 17th Street, NEW YORK.   122 and 124 Wabash Avenue, CHICAGO

1891.

Figure 2.8.   Title Page from John W. Tufts and H. E. Holt, *the Normal Music Course, Second Reader* (Boston: Silver, Burdett & Co., 1891).

wanted to be sure that its purpose would be educational. Educators were not satisfied when students sang well but did not master music reading. The three part rationale of the 1830s that had supported music education still prevailed; school systems adopted music as a scientific subject that promised mental, physical, and moral benefits for pupils. A scientific approach to music instruction required a scientific method, and the new graded series of music texts was based solidly on music reading.

The authors of the most significant series of this era, *The Normal Music Course*, were Hosea Holt (1836–1898) and John Tufts (1825–1908). Holt was a Boston woodturner and singing school master, and served as a bandsman during the Civil War. He had studied with Benjamin Baker and later taught music at Wheaton Seminary and Bridgewater Normal School. Holt joined the music staff of the Boston schools in 1869 and remained there for the rest of his life.

The Normal Music Course was published originally by D. Appleton and Company in 1883. Edgar Silver purchased the rights in 1885 and entered the field of music education with it. Silver's company later became Silver, Burdett & Company (John 1954, 110). The series consisted of five books that emphasized sight-singing exercises. The part exercises were contrapuntal, giving every voice a melody to sing, and exercise material was incorporated into the songs. Supplementary music for *The Normal Music Course* was published in a serial pamphlet entitled *The Coda*, which cost three cents per copy. Like *The National Music Series,* large charts accompanied *The Normal Music Course.*

The authors regarded sight-singing as the only means by which students could truly understand music:

> Sight-reading alone is not the object of the Normal Music Course. Through sight-reading a way is opened to the knowledge of music, and the Readers are offered as illustrations and suggestions in harmony and rhythm. This is more easily effected by careful study of the component melodies. Let each melody be carefully sung until it becomes familiar, the various combinations of the parts can then be produced and the resulting harmonies critically examined. It is not intended by this that the student shall become expert in the use of technical terms, but that the education of the ear may be gained by the *production* of these sounds in combination. By this course the ear receives its best training, and the effect will be lasting. (*School Music Monthly* 1903, 11)

The Normal Music Course became the standard for school music series by 1893, and many subsequent series were based on the note reading method (John, 114).

Figure 2.9. Pages 28 and 29 of *The Normal Music Course, Second Reader.*

Publishers' Schools

Holt established a summer school in Lexington, Massachusetts, to introduce *The Normal Music Course*. Its emphasis on teaching methodology made it unique among all of the summer institutes that covered church music and vocal pedagogy. The summer school's success led Luther Whiting Mason's publisher, Ginn and Company, to establish a school of its own, the National Summer School of Music, to promote *The National Music Course*. Silver, Burdett and Ginn later opened western branches in Chicago for *The New National Music Course* and in Lake Geneva, Wisconsin, for *The Normal Music Course*. Silver's school moved to Chicago in 1891, where it was incorporated by Silver, Burdett & Company and renamed the American Institute of Normal Methods. Both schools based their curricula on the school music books of their respective owners, and they also taught music appreciation, theory, melodic interpretation, and conducting. The National Summer School of Music operated for more than a quarter of a century and closed only when public normal schools and colleges began to train school music teachers.

Other Series

In 1860, Cincinnati music teachers produced *The Young Singer* for the Board of Education, and *The Young Singer's Manual* in 1866. Later, they wrote several editions of the *Cincinnati Music Readers,* which were used in many other cities. The last revision was by Gustave Junkermann in 1893. *The Cincinnati Music Readers* demonstrate that the teaching of music reading was taken seriously in the last third of the nineteenth century. Cincinnati's music exhibit at the 1876 Centennial Exposition in Philadelphia consisted of the charts used for oral examinations of schoolchildren and their written examinations. They were extraordinary enough to be displayed in Paris two years later at the exhibition that featured the Trocadero buildings.

The Natural Music Course (American Book Company, 1895), by Thomas Tapper and Frederick Ripley, was the outstanding series published at the end of the last decade of the nineteenth century. Tapper was an authority on music teaching, and Ripley was headmaster of a Boston school. They recognized that so many gimmicks and devices had accumulated in school music series that a straightforward method was needed. *The Natural Music Course* was appreciated for its simplicity. It also contained some new

THE

CINCINNATI

MUSIC READER.

COMPLETE.

A

COLLECTION OF EXERCISES AND SONGS,

IN ONE & TWO PARTS,

FOR GRADES H, G, F, E AND D.

PREPARED AT THE REQUEST OF THE

BOARD OF EDUCATION

BY THE

TEACHERS OF MUSIC.

Published by

JOHN CHURCH & CO.,

66 WEST FOURTH ST., CINCINNATI.

Figure 2.10. Title page of *The Cincinnati Music Reader, texts in English and German* (Cincinnati: John Church & Co., 1875).

and innovative approaches to simplify music instruction. Ripley discussed the series almost twenty years later:

> I concluded that the one vital idea . . . contained in Mr. Holt's repeated assertion [was] that real musicianship was based on the perception of tone relations as a perfectly definite thing. All the rest went by the board. Having reached this conclusion I set myself the task of devising a presentation of music which should be entirely free of technicalities, so called, but which should make the notation as it now exists an actual, vital expression of a real thing to all pupils who beheld it. Definition and theory were entirely eliminated. Numbers, hand signs, ladders and the like were omitted. Rhythm was joined to melody, and the interval as a study disappeared from elementary work. All representations were musical and complete. (Ripley 1917, 94–104)

The same authors published the *Harmonic Course in Music* in 1903 and the *Melodic Course in Music* in 1906.[8]

William Tomlins, in turn, focused on beautiful singing. He came to Chicago from England in 1870 and started as the director of a sixty voice male chorus that grew to four hundred when he changed it to a mixed group. Around 1890, he began to work with children's groups and to train teachers for the Chicago Board of Education. The children's chorus that he directed at the Columbian Exposition in 1893 was so well received that his work became the standard for teaching children to sing. Striving for beautiful song became a method in its own right, using techniques from both the reading and rote approaches but focusing on tone. Tomlins was the editor of C. C. Birchard's *Laurel Series*, copyrighted in 1900, which provided folk and composed song literature of high quality.

Twentieth Century Series

The Ripley and Tapper *Revised Natural Music Series*, published in 1903, continued a traditional approach to music reading, although it was more interesting to children than many of its competitors. The same was true of Ginn's *The New Educational Music Course* (1906) by James McLaughlin and W. W. Gilchrist. However, publishers were cautious. Silver, Burdett & Company had moved in a new direction with the Smith and Foresman *Modern Music Series*, but reversed itself in 1910 with the *Normal Music*

---

8. It is ironic that books intended to eliminate gimmicks should be named after the three modes of the minor scale without revealing whether the titles themselves were a gimmick.

Course, a revision of the Holt and Tufts work by Samuel Cole and Leonard B. Marshall. This series continued the subject-centered approach of the original (Growman 1985, 97).

The American Book Company asked Smith and Foresman to prepare a new set of books to capitalize on their earlier success. From 1908 to 1911, they produced the six-volume *Eleanor Smith Music Course.*

Nineteenth century educators used the word "science" to mean modern. The key word in the early part of the twentieth century was "progressive," as in Theodore Roosevelt's political party. *The Progressive Music Series,* by Osbourne McConathy, Edward Bailey Birge, and W. Otto Miessner was first published in 1914. Horatio Parker, dean of the Yale School of Music, whose opera *Mona* had just won a Metropolitan Opera prize, was included among the authors. McConathy was senior editor and Birge and Miessner contributed songs related to each new musical concept. Themes from Mozart, Beethoven, and Dvořák in the texts were related to musical elements experienced in singing. Teacher's manuals emphasized the sequential nature of the learning activities. The series was widely adopted.

Other publishers met the challenge of *The Progressive Music Series* slowly. The American Book Company had released the first book in the *Hollis Dann Music Course* in 1912. It emphasized tone, rhythm, and musical dictation. The Dann series included many interesting songs, but music reading was still its primary emphasis. The American Book Company's commitment to the Dann series and the Smith books kept it from responding with a truly new entry for thirty years. In 1920, Hinds, Hayden, and Eldridge produced *The Universal Music Series,* edited by Karl Gehrkens, George Gartlan, and Walter Damrosch. The objective of the series was to instill a love of music. Free rhythmic interpretation allowed the children to be creative. The series incorporated music history, analysis, and listening.

Songs of Childhood, the first book of Ginn and Company's *Music Education Series,* appeared in 1923. It was prepared by leaders of the Music Supervisors National Conference. The editors were Will Earhart, T. P. Giddings, and Ralph Baldwin. Like the "progressive" books, there were no musical exercises, but students were encouraged to look for motives rather than read from note to note, and eurhythmics was introduced. Appreciation was a major goal, and a series of phonograph records keyed to the student books accompanied the books. Melody writing provided the opportunity to experience the creative joy of music.

In addition to these textbook series, a number of songbooks appeared, and some provided musical material of exceptionally high quality: Alys Bentley's *The Song Series* (A. S. Barnes, 1907, 1910), William L. Tomlins's

The Laurel Song-Reader (Birchard, 1914), and *The Foresman Book of Songs* (American Book Company, 1925–1926). Charles Fullerton's *One Book Course*, with accompanying records, was designed for rural schools: it brought music to those schools years earlier than might have been otherwise possible in many areas of the country.

In the 1920s, Silver, Burdett published an enlarged edition of some of the *Progressive* books. At the same time, Ginn planned a new series to be known as *The World of Music*. Its principal editor was Mabelle Glenn, who was assisted by Helen Leavitt, Victor Rebmann, and Earl Baker. Glenn had observed instruction in Dalcroze eurhythmics at an international conference in Lausanne, Switzerland, and she incorporated similar ideas in her approach to reading rhythms. She also keyed twelve common melodic patterns to songs in the second grade book, which gave children a basis for elementary music reading and creating. Two-color illustrations and a few art masterpieces in four colors made the books attractive. Harold Rugg, of Columbia University Teachers College, helped integrate the songs with other subjects.

Thaddeus P. Giddings

Thaddeus Giddings was a Midwesterner who believed in teaching children to read music by having them read through as many songs as possible. A condensed form of the practice he instituted in Minneapolis, and possibly earlier in Oak Park, Illinois, follows:

First Grade: As many as 100 songs taught by rote. Second Grade: *Two* weeks of reviewing songs known. Assigned good singers to back row so others always had a better tone to which to listen. *Third* week, syllables taught to six or seven familiar songs. *Circa Seventh* week, teacher seated in front of the children who sing a familiar song slowly with syllables. Repeats it more slowly; and again, more slowly. On the fourth time the teacher stops them on a tone and has them sing the tone several times; then they sing *do*. Then each of the tones of the scale was presented in the song and compared with *do*, then with each other and it sometimes happened, in a room where the attention was good, that all the tones were learned in twenty minutes. . . . When a tone was forgotten, it was not given by the teacher but the school were told to sing the song until they came to that tone. The activity was repeated the next day and by the end of the week individuals were trying the skips. Much individual work followed. *Eighth* week the children are shown the song in the book, following which the teacher, using whole notes, put the notes on a blackboard staff as children sing song. When it is fully displayed children sing tones as teacher points to various notes. Then students drew notes on board as teacher sang. *Ninth* week, books distributed to children. (Giddings 1908, 29–30)

William A. Hodgdon

William A. Hodgdon was one of the early music teachers to combine elements of the song method with other approaches. Hodgdon, a student of Lowell Mason and George Webb, taught in Fort Wayne, Indiana, and Saint Louis after the Civil War. His plan of instruction was based on a repertoire of twenty songs, some of them his own compositions. He led a chorus of 3,500 Saint Louis schoolchildren that he prepared for the 1903 National Song Festival of the North American Singing Society and was the music organizer of the Saint Louis World's Fair the next year (Suehs 1971, 37–38).

High School Music

The high school was the last segment of the public school system to be established. Common school education in many American communities, especially rural areas and small towns, ended with the eighth grade until well after the Civil War. The 1860 census listed only 350 public high schools, mostly in northern cities where full twelve-year programs were first developed. Vocal music was part of the high school curriculum from the beginning, and the curriculum usually consisted of singing the choruses of European masters. Charles Aiken's *High School Choralist* (1866) and *The Choralist's Companion* (1872) contained four part choral works by Handel, Haydn, Mozart, Beethoven, Mendelssohn, Silcher, Barnby, Dr. Calcott, Meyerbeer, Spohr, Rossini, and Mehul.

In schools that were large enough, senior classes provided music for their own graduation ceremonies. In cities like Worcester, Massachusetts, and Cincinnati, Ohio, the high schools became the training ground for community festival choruses that established international reputations. By the end of the century, production of operettas also became an established tradition in some schools. A few schools were even able to present full oratorios, although the supervisors or professional singers usually sang the major solos.

Teacher Training

Normal schools began in Lexington, Massachusetts, in 1839 and came into their own after the Civil War. They played a major role in professionalizing teaching in the common schools. Most of the normal schools were established by the states, but there were many private institutions, and some cities had their own training centers. A normal school became a permanent part of the Cincinnati school system in 1868. Saint Louis had a normal school that prepared classroom teachers to teach music. It became a teachers' college named after the former superintendent of the city schools, William Torrey Harris, in the first decade of the twentieth century. Harris had established the first public kindergarten in the United States and was United States Commissioner of Education from 1889 to 1906.

The grade school teachers who enrolled in most of the normal schools had instruction in vocal music, but music supervisors did not attend them until Julia Ettie Crane opened the Potsdam (New York) Musical Institute in 1884. She offered her music students authentic teaching experience in a model classroom of the Normal School at Potsdam. Her curriculum for the public school offered a compromise in the "rote-note" disagreement, as she instructed her students to develop listening skills and musical memory in the younger children, and to delay sight-reading until the grammar grades. Crane was firmly committed to musicianship and to pedagogy in training supervisors. She helped balance the curriculum of future music educators.

In the 1880s, candidates for music specialist positions in public schools were still examined only in music. Even when the theory and practice of teaching was included in the examinations, most of the candidates were products of music schools rather than teacher training institutions. Joseph Surdo, who began teaching in Cincinnati in 1891 after two years at the College of Music, was told to prepare for the pedagogy part of the examination by visiting the schools to see how school music teaching was done (Surdo 1950).[9]

Two kinds of teacher preparation institutions held opposing philosophies of how music teachers should be educated. Julia Etta Crane, who had graduated from Potsdam Normal School in 1874, wanted to provide music to all children. The faculties of colleges and conservatories, however, considered music an elite art not to be wasted on the untalented. Their graduates were unlikely to be comfortable as school music supervisors.

Summer Schools

Music summer schools served a real need as music became a regular subject of study in many schools. Neither the colleges nor the normal schools

---

9. The tests probably were not demanding. Elwood Cubberly reported in the *National Society for the Study of Education Yearbook* of 1906 that an eleven-year-old boy received a mark of 98 percent on a county teacher test.

had developed early training programs for music supervisors. The summer schools sponsored by the book companies continued to be the major source of trained supervisors for at least twenty-five years. The American Book Company established the New School of Methods in Chicago with Thomas Tapper as principal. The Emma Thomas School opened in Detroit. Ginn and Company hired Enos Pearson, a music supervisor in New Hampshire, to head a summer school to operate in cooperation with Plymouth Normal School. Other summer schools were established by conservatories.

Many twentieth century music education leaders were teachers or students in the summer schools. Osbourne McConathy assisted Luther Whiting Mason with the National Summer School and took over the leadership role when Mason died in 1896. Both Hollis Dann and Walter Aiken were on the faculty of the American Book Company's New School of Methods under the direction of Thomas Tapper. Ralph Baldwin assisted Sterrie A. Weaver and eventually directed the Institute of Music Pedagogy in Northampton, Massachusetts. C. C. Birchard managed the Emma Thomas School, where Frances E. Clark trained to be a supervisor and Peter Dykema attended as a boy observer (Clark 1924, 603–11).

Friedrich Wilhelm Froebel

Friedrich Froebel, a student of Pestalozzi, held that the teacher drew knowledge from the child, and so the teacher's role was to devise ways to help the child voluntarily engage in meaningful activity. He believed that each stage of life was built on the previous one. He created the kindergarten because the early stage of life influenced the rest of the child's life. The kindergarten was expected to provide opportunity for creative self-involvement for children not yet of school age.

Mrs. Carl Schurz opened a kindergarten for German-speaking children in Wisconsin in 1856, and Elizabeth Peabody founded a private kindergarten in Boston in the 1860s. The first American kindergarten connected with a public school system was established in Saint Louis in 1873. Music played an important role in the growth of the kindergarten movement. *The Kindergarten Songbook* was one of the principal vehicles for the spread of the kindergarten influence (Vandewalken 1907, 24). Eleanor Smith dedicated her significant publication, *Songs for Little Children*, "To Chicago Kindergarteners [*sic*], and to all lovers of Children Everywhere" (Smith 1887, frontispiece).

Colonel Francis W. Parker was an innovative educator whose ideas had proven successful in the Quincy and Boston, Massachusetts, schools. He

THE AMERICAN INSTITUTE OF NORMAL METHODS

STUDENT'S REGISTRY BLANK

DEPARTMENT OF VOCAL MUSIC

.................................{ Eastern or / Western } School, Session of 19

Date,............................19

Name in full,...

Permanent P. O. Address, Town or City...

Street and Number,...............................County, ...State, ...

P. O. Address *for the coming year*, if not as above,..

1. Age.............................. 2. Married or unmarried?...............................

3. What previous sessions of this Institute have you attended?.................................

4. What other advantages and TRAINING IN VOCAL MUSIC have you had by way of preparation for teaching it?...
....

5. Have you had experience as a SPECIAL TEACHER OF MUSIC?.....................If so, where, and how many years in each place?..
....

6. Have you done GRADE WORK in Music?........ ....
Where?.............................In what Grades?.................................

7. State fully your qualifications and experience, if any, in TEACHING INSTRUMENTAL MUSIC,.............
....

8. State your general educational advantages and training, OUTSIDE OF MUSIC,.........................
....

9. Are you qualified to do HIGH SCHOOL work, outside of Music?...................................

10. Could you, if necessary, teach Penmanship, Drawing, Physical Training, or Pianoforte in addition to Vocal Music?...

11. What other branches could you teach?........ ....
....

12. Do you care to teach any of the above in connection with Vocal Music?...........................

13. What experience, if any, have you had in teaching other branches than Music? (Give full particulars.)
....
....

14. What is the compass and quality of your voice?...

15. What experience, if any, have you had as church organist, or singer?...............................

16. Would you like to fill such a position in addition to your teaching?................................

17. What are your church preferences?..............18. Have you a position for next year?............

19. As a special or as a grade teacher?..........................20. Where?..............

21. At what salary?....... 22. How much of your time does the work occupy?.......................

23. If a position for next year is desired, what location or section of country do you prefer?.............

24. What salary do you desire?...............25. What is the lowest salary you would accept?.........

26. Do you intend to complete the course in this school to graduation?...............................

Give, on the back of this sheet, names of persons to whom you would refer for testimonials as to your ability, experience and training. File with this blank any testimonials you have with you, and your photograph.

N. B.—It is earnestly desired that every member of the school fill out this blank at the opening of the session. As these records are carefully preserved for the benefit of the pupils, the propriety and advantage of answering each question explicitly are evident. Students are requested to read these questions through carefully before beginning to answer them.

Figure 2.11. Student's registry blank form for The American Institute of Normal Methods.

regarded the education of the whole child to be a fundamental principle, and he believed that true learning occurred only through self-generated activity. Parker's interest in the whole person led him to the belief that, while music training incorporated intellectual and disciplinary aspects, its true and unique contribution was in the realm of the emotions. The view of music as trainer of the emotions was not accepted by the majority of music educators until well into the twentieth century. Even then, many thought that teaching children to read music took precedence over any other objective.

Practicing the new psychology, Parker and other education leaders reversed the process. The new music teacher sought ways to replace years of joyless drill with deeply moving musical experiences. These experiences were expected to motivate children to develop the skills that would allow them to enjoy music throughout their lifetimes. The term *progressive education* became synonymous with the entire movement to change the practices of the traditional school, although no official organization was formed until 1919. By that time, John Dewey had developed a philosophy and a theory of education that came to represent progressivism in the minds of most people.

The New Education and Music

John Dewey moved from the University of Chicago to Teachers College, Columbia University, in 1904. He was the acknowledged leader of the child study movement that G. Stanley Hall had set in motion. Both men favored music education and spoke about the role it could play in the school. Music fit comfortably into the new education because it required physical demonstrations of what students learned. Especially meaningful for music education was Dewey's statement that appeared in *Moral Principles in Education*: "Who can reckon up the loss of moral power that arises from the constant impression that nothing is worth doing in itself, but only as a preparation for something else." Music educators were grateful for the support of an esteemed education figure like Dewey. The innovative *Progressive Music Series* became available to the schools five years before the Progressive Education Association was founded. Many experiments related to the new thinking made significant use of music.

Americans were comfortable with teaching children to read music and singing patriotic songs, but were suspicious of sensitizing children to beautiful sound and color. They were mistrustful about teaching methods that allowed children to decide for themselves what they would do on a given day. Dewey's pragmatism fit in with the "can do" attitude of the frontier, but many of the subtleties of the new relationship between teacher and learner did not. Often, the teachers did not change the atmosphere of their classrooms, despite the benefits of workshops, graduate study, lectures, and demonstrations at Music Supervisors National Conference, and other professional meetings (Mark and Gary 2007, 224). Despite notable successes, progressive education did not achieve wide acceptance, although many of its concepts permeated American education.

Many practitioners of psychology as a science were interested in music, and some music educators became so engrossed in the problems of learning music that they became psychologists themselves. James L. Mursell was the most influential music educator to do so. Two of his books published in the 1930s, *The Psychology of School Music Teaching* (with Kansas City music supervisor Mabelle Glenn) and *Human Values and Music Education*, became standard texts.

The State of Music Education: Two Surveys

John Eaton, Commissioner of the United States Bureau of Education from 1870 to 1886, was encouraged by Theodore Presser to survey the status of music in American schools in 1886. The survey requested the following information from public school systems throughout the United States:

> Is music taught? In what grades? By special teacher? By regular teacher? By both regular and special teachers? Number of hours per week? Please state what, if any, instrument is used to lead the singing. Which system is used of the three commonly known as "fixed *do*," "movable *do*," or "tonic *sol-fa*," or are different ones used in different schools? If different systems are used, which finds most favor? What text-books or charts are used? Are there stated musical examinations, or exhibitions, or both? Is notation required in music books? Please send copy of regulations, if any have been printed. Please state, if possible, whether any established vocal societies (independent of church choirs) are now in active operation in your city; if so, please give names of societies and full addresses of conductors. If music is not taught in your schools, what objections, if any, would probably be urged against the introduction of systematic instruction in it? (Bergee 1987, 107)

The survey revealed that public school music was not yet widely accepted. Only 250 school systems indicated that music was being taught regularly. The fact that the survey was carried out, however, and especially by the federal government, showed that school music was gathering strength.

The National Education Association

In 1889, the Department of Music Education of the National Education Association approved a resolution to collect data on music instruction throughout the United States. An appropriation of $100 was approved to conduct the study by means of a questionnaire sent to the state and county superintendents, and the superintendents or secretaries of school boards of the larger American cities. The responses indicated that music instruction had increased since the 1886 survey, and that administrators in all parts of the country were favorable toward it. Only four superintendents expressed negative opinions about music instruction. The report stated that music "had withstood the crucial test of experience and critical observation," and that "music should be regularly and systematically taught in the schools." Again, the rationale for this statement was the same used by the Boston School Committee a half century earlier—intellectual, moral, and physical development (Silver 1889, 684–93).

TOPICS FOR THOUGHT AND DISCUSSION

1. In what ways did Pestalozzi influence American education? Music education?
2. William Channing Woodbridge was not a music educator, but he was one of the most vocal supporters of it. Why?
3. What direction might music education have taken if Lowell Mason had never become involved in promoting it?
4. What was the historic importance of the normal institutes?
5. Why is Cincinnati mentioned so prominently in this chapter?
6. Why were music educators called supervisors? What was their role in the classroom?
7. Why was the latter part of the nineteenth century a period of maturation for the music education profession?

REFERENCES

Bergee, Martin. Summer 1987. "Ringing the Changes: General John Eaton and the 1886 Public School Music Survey." *Journal of Research in Music Education* 35.

Birge, Edward Bailey. 1928. *History of Public School Music in the United States.* Washington, DC: Music Educators National Conference.

Board of Trustees. 1838. *Minutes of the Board of Trustees and Visitors of Common Schools.* 1838. Cincinnati, June 18, vol. 1.

Boston Musical Gazette, *Devoted to the Science of Music,* December 5, 12, 1838. Report completed in December 26, 1836 edition.

Brayley, A. W. 1905. *The Musician,* reported in Edward Bailey Birge, *History of Public School Music in the United States.* Washington, DC: Music Educators National Conference.

Britton, Allen P. 1961. "Music Education: An American Specialty." In *One Hundred Years of Music in America,* ed. Paul Henry Lang. New York: Schirmer.

Buttelman, C. V. 1937. "A Century of Music in Buffalo Schools." *Music Educators Journal* 23.

Cincinnati Daily Gazette, April 16, 1834: 7; October 3, 1838: 2.

Clark, Frances Elliott. "School Music in 1836, 1886, 1911, and 1936." 1924. *Proceedings of the National Education Association.*

Cuban, Larry. 1984. *How Teachers Taught: Constancy and Change in American Classrooms, 1890–1980.* New York: Longman.

Dejarnette, Reven S. 1940. *Hollis Dann: His Life and Contributions to Music Education.* Boston: C. C. Birchard.

Efland, Arthur. Fall 1983. "Art and Music in the Pestalozzian Tradition." *Journal of Research in Music Education* 31.

Eightieth Annual Report of the Public Schools of Cincinnati for the School Year Ending August 31, 1909. Cincinnati, Ohio.

Ellis, H. Spring 1955. "Lowell Mason and the Manual of the Boston Academy of Music." *Journal of Research in Music Education* 3.

Elson, Louis C. 1915. *The History of American Music.* New York: Macmillan.

Flueckiger, Samuel L. February 1936. "Why Lowell Mason Left the Boston Schools." *Music Educators Journal.*

Gary, Charles L. 1954. "A History of Music Education in the Cincinnati Public Schools." *Journal of Research in Music Education* 2.

Giddings, Thaddeus P. May 1908. "Song Method." *School Music,* 9.

Gould, Nathaniel D. 1853. *Church Music in America.* Boston: A. N. Johnson.

Growman, Florence. 1985. "The Emergence of the Concept of General Music as Reflected in Basal Textbooks 1900–1980." DMA dissertation, The Catholic University of America.

Gutek, Gerald Lee. 1978. *Joseph Neef, The Americanization of Pestalozzianism.* University, AL: University of Alabama Press.

Hartley, Kenneth Ray. 1960. "A Study of the Life and Works of Luther Whiting Mason." EdD dissertation, Florida State University.

John, Robert. Fall 1954. "Nineteenth Century Graded Vocal Series." *Journal of Research in Music Education* 2.

———. Spring 1960. "Elam Ives and the Pestalozzian Philosophy of Music Education." *Journal of Research in Music Education* 8.

———. Winter 1965. "Origins of the First Music Educators Convention." *Journal of Research in Music Education* 13.

Jorgensen, Estelle R. Spring 1983. "Engineering Change in Music Education: A Model of the Political Process Underlying the Boston School Music Movement (1829–1838)." *Journal of Research in Music Education* 31.

Kapfer, Miriam B. 1967. "Early Public School Music in Columbus, 1845–1854." *Journal of Research in Music Education* 15.

Keating, Mary. 1989. "Lowell Mason in Savannah." *Bulletin of Historical Research in Music Education.*

Keene, James A. 1982. *A History of Music Education in the United States.* Hanover, NH: University Press of New England.

Lang, Paul Henry, ed. 1961. "Music Education: An American Specialty," in *One Hundred Years of Music in America.* New York: Schirmer, 10.

Mark, Michael L. 1984. "Pestalozzi and 19th Century Music Education." *International Journal of Music Education* 3.

———. 2007. *Music Education: Source Readings from Ancient Greece to Today,* third edition. New York: Routledge.

Mark, Michael L., and Charles L. Gary. 2007. *A History of American Music Education,* third edition. Lanham, MD: Rowman & Littlefield Education.

Mason, Lowell. 1843. *Manual of the Boston Academy of Music for Instruction in the Elements of Vocal Music on the System of Pestalozzi.* Boston: Carter, Hendee.

Mason, Luther Whiting. 1870. *Second Music Reader: A Course of Exercises in the Elements of Vocal Music and Sight-Singing, with Choice Rote Songs for the Use of Schools and Families.* Boston: Ginn Brothers.

Minutes of the Board of Trustees and Visitors of Common Schools, Cincinnati, January 21, 1856, vol. 7; June 27, 1853, vol. 6; March 2, 1857, vol. 7.

"Music in the Common Schools." *American Annals of Education and Instruction,* July 1831: 1.

Pemberton, Carol A. 1985. *Lowell Mason: His Life and Work.* Ann Arbor, MI: UMI Research Press.

———. January 1990. "A Look at *The Juvenile Lyre* (1831): Posing a Rationale for Music in the Schools." *Bulletin of Historical Research in Music Education* 11.

Perham, Beatrice. 1937. *Music in the New School.* Chicago: Neil A. Kjos Co.

Perkins, S. May 1908. "Reminiscences of Early Days in School Music." *School Music* 9.

Raynor, Henry. 1878. *Music and Society since 1815.* New York: Taplinger.

Rich, Arthur L. 1946. *Lowell Mason: The Father of Singing among the Children.* Chapel Hill: University of North Carolina Press.

Rideout, Roger R. Fall 1982. "On Early Applications of Psychology in Music Education." *Journal of Research in Music Education* 30.

Ripley, F. H. 1917. "How to Promote Musical Appreciation without Technical Work." *MTNA Proceedings* 29:94–104.

School Committee. 1837. "Report." *Boston Musical Gazette: Devoted to the Science of Music.* December 5, 12.

School Music Monthly, May 1903: 4; June 1904: 5.

Silver, Edgar O. 1889. "Special Report on the Condition of Music Instruction in the Public Schools of the United States." *National Education Association Proceedings.*

Smith, Eleanor. 1887. *Songs for Little Children.* Springfield, MA: Milton Bradley.

Stowe, C. E. Stowe. 1838. "Report on the Course of Instruction in the Common Schools of Prussia and Wurtemberg." *Transactions of the Seventh Annual Meeting of the Western Literary Society and College of Professional Teachers.* Cincinnati: James H. Allbach.

Suehs, Hermann C. 1971. "The Legacy of William Augustus Hodgdon, School Music Teacher." Diss., Catholic University of America.

Sunderman, Lloyd F. 1956. "The Era of Beginnings in American Music Education (1830–1840)." *Journal of Research in Music Education* 3.

———. 1971. *Historical Foundations of Music Education in the United States.* Metuchen, NJ: Scarecrow Press.

Surdo, Joseph. 1950. Interview with Charles L. Gary. September 3. Norwood, OH.

Tufts, John. 1894. *Normal Music Course: A Series of Exercises, Studies, and Songs, Defining and Illustrating the Art of Sight Reading; Progressively Arranged from the First Conception and Production of Tones to the Most Advanced Choral Practice,* Introductory Third Reader. Boston: Silver, Burdett & Company.

Vandewalken, Nina C. 1907. "The History of the Kindergarten Influence in Elementary Education." *Sixth Yearbook.* Chicago: National Society for the Study of Education.

Wilson, Bruce. 1973. "A Documentary History of Music in the Public Schools of the City of Boston, 1830–1850." PhD dissertation, University of Michigan.

3

PROFESSIONAL EDUCATION
ORGANIZATIONS

Horace Mann was the first president of the American Association for the Advancement of Education, founded in 1848. In 1859, the organization merged with the National Teachers Association (NTA), founded a year earlier. In 1879, two other organizations, the National Association of School Superintendents and the American Normal School Association, joined the NTA to create the National Education Association (NEA).

Many of the superintendents and principals of normal schools at the early NEA meetings had experience with strong music programs. Daniel B. Hagar, head of the Salem, Massachusetts, Normal School, was an early leader of the normal school group that made music an important part of their meeting agendas. Eben Tourjée, of the Conservatory of Music in Boston, gave a major address entitled "A Plea for Vocal Music in the Public Schools." He called for music to be "a strong educational appliance coordinated in rank with the other studies . . . to be pursued as systematically and thoroughly as they." Tourjée cited the practical, moral, aesthetic, and religious benefits of music to children. "Sculpture, painting and architecture may charm, may elevate, but music softens, thrills, subdues. It quickens the whole range of emotions. For each it has a voice, of each it is the interpreter. Sown in the heart of youth, its influence blesses his whole life" (Barnard and Bardeen 1909, 799–813).

At the 1872 Boston meeting, J. C. Greenough, principal of the State Normal School in Providence, spoke of music in schools as a means of aesthetic culture. J. B. Buchanan of Kentucky delivered a major address entitled "Full-Orbed Education" at the NEA meeting in Minneapolis in 1875. He discussed the value of music in education and mentioned that Wesleyan University President Joseph Cummings had expressed similar

thoughts at an earlier meeting. Music education clearly had influential supporters in the early years of the NEA.

THE DEPARTMENT OF MUSIC EDUCATION

After the Department of Art was created at the 1883 meeting, President T.
W. Valentine suggested to Luther Whiting Mason and Theodore F. Seward
that they encourage vocal music teachers to attend the next NEA meeting
in Madison, Wisconsin, where a petition to create the Department of Music
Education was to be approved. Discussions of music education and singing
demonstrations by school children became regular parts of subsequent NEA
meetings. Many of the presentations at the department meetings dealt with
singing, and new ideas began to be discussed at the turn of the century.
Samuel W. Cole said in his speech at the 1903 meeting in Boston:

> What then is the purpose of teaching music in the public schools? I an-
> swer: the creation of a musical atmosphere in America; the establishment
> of a musical environment in every home; the development of a national
> type of music. . . . In short, the real purpose of teaching music in the
> schools is to lay the foundation for all that we can hope or wish to realize,
> musically, in the United States of America. . . . To sum it all up: the real
> purpose of teaching music in the public schools is not to make expert
> sight-singers nor individual soloists. I speak from experience. I have done
> all these things, and I can do them again; but I have learned that, if they
> become an end and not a means, they hinder rather than help. . . . A
> much nobler, grander, more inspiring privilege is yours and mine: to get
> the great mass to singing and to make them love it. (*Journal of Proceedings
> and Addresses of the National Education Association* 1903, 605–99)

COOPERATIVE EFFORTS

The NEA absorbed education associations that represented many aspects
of public education—administration at every level, subject-oriented specialists, the improvement of teacher education, curriculum development,
education technology, and various school services.

Most came together in the late 1950s in their new home, the
$6,000,000 NEA Building at 16th Street NW, in Washington, DC, built
entirely with member contributions. The editor of *The NEA Journal* regularly consulted with those in the NEA building to be sure the magazine was

in step with all aspects of public education. In 1963, the NEA Research Department produced *Music and Art in the Schools*, which provided a clear picture of the status of the two disciplines.

In the 1970s, competition for members with the American Federation of Teachers, a trade union of the AFL-CIO, led the NEA to abandon the role of a professional association. It gave up its tax-exempt status as a not-for-profit organization and became a labor union. As a result, it was permitted to lobby Congress for the direct welfare of its members. A major effect of this move was that several organizations of administrators were considered management and had to leave the NEA building. The Music Educators National Conference left because its purpose was not compatible with that of a labor union.

The relationship had been fruitful because NEA had forced school boards throughout the country to hire thousands of teachers of art, music, and physical education to create preparation time for classroom teachers. That substantially increased the amount of time for music instruction, and school systems that had reduced elementary music programs during the Great Depression and World War II were forced to reinstate them.

The Music Teachers National Association

In 1875, Eben Tourjée, former Director of the New England Conservatory of Music, organized a summer school in East Greenwich, Rhode Island. Among the music teachers he attracted were three Ohioans, N. Coe Stewart and William Henry Dana of Akron and Theodore Presser, professor of piano at Ohio Female Seminary in Delaware, Ohio. These three, and G. M. Cole of Richmond, Indiana, persuaded Theodore Presser to host a convention of teachers in Delaware the following year. That convention evolved into the Music Teachers National Association (MTNA), the first permanent association of musicians in the United States.

MTNA focused on private instruction from the beginning. William Henry Dana spoke at the 1914 meeting about the condition of private instruction in the United States. He commented on the young women who taught piano for "pin money" without having become competent as pianists. He said that voice teachers were, "for the most part, charlatans or broken down opera singers." It was these conditions, he said, that "called into existence the Music Teachers National Association." Most who came to the first meeting were private teachers of piano, organ, and voice. School music leaders George F. Root and Luther Whiting Mason from Boston, George Loomis from Indianapolis, N. Coe Stewart from Cleveland, and his former student Nathan Glover from Akron also attended. The hosts, Theodore Presser and E. Z. Lorenz, were to become publishers.

The MTNA membership represented two factions: one dedicated to well-educated private teachers; the other comprising those interested in school music (who were called the Do-Re-Mi fraternity). Antagonism between these factions helped drive school music teachers away from the organization. Despite their differences, the two groups sometimes cooperated on projects of common interest, including the support of copyright law revision.

The American Association of School Administrators

During the 1865 meeting of the National Teachers Association in Harrisburg, Pennsylvania, a group of state and city superintendents agreed to form an organization for administrators. They adopted the name National Association of School Superintendents the following year at the NTA meeting, but it was renamed the Department of School Superintendence of the National Education Association in 1870. The current name, American Association of School Administrators, was adopted in 1932. It was still a department of the NEA at that time.

Many leaders of AASA helped advance the cause of music education. Randall J. Condon, superintendent of the Cincinnati schools from 1913 to 1929, addressed the music educators at their 1922 meeting in Nashville (Condon 1922, 34–37), and again when they met in Cincinnati in 1924. When he became president of the Department of Superintendence, he was responsible for preparing the 1927 annual meeting (Aiken 1926). Condon was impressed by Joseph Maddy's Richmond, Indiana, high school orchestra when it performed at the convention. He asked his own director of music, Walter Aiken, to arrange for Maddy and the newly created National High School Orchestra to perform for the superintendents in Dallas.

The concert was the first exposure that most of the superintendents had had to excellent music performed by students. They were inspired, and they took their enthusiasm home to school systems all over the country. The Dallas program was filled with singing, bands, and smaller ensembles. This experience gave Maddy the confidence to go forward with the National High School Orchestra Camp, which he and Thaddeus P. Giddings founded the next year at Interlochen, Michigan.

In 1927, members of the Music Education Research Council of the Music Supervisors National Conference joined with superintendents Philander P. Claxton of Tulsa, Jesse H. Newlon of Denver, Herbert S. Weet of Rochester, and Thomas Finnegan of Harrisburg to discuss school music. One of their resolutions was to immediately extend music study to all rural schools. Joseph Maddy wrote: "As the result of this 'musical crusade' the convention passed a resolution placing music on an equal basis with the other fundamental subjects in education—the greatest victory for music in the history of the nation" (Maddy 1929, 203).

Two years later the superintendents passed another resolution calling for a study "looking toward re-evaluating the arts with a view to assigning them more fundamental recognition in the programs of high schools and colleges" (Music Supervisors National Conference 1929, 57).

Condon continued his close association with the music educators. He said at the 1929 meeting of the Music Supervisors National Conference in Philadelphia:

> First, beauty—music and art and drama—is most fundamental to education and unless we begin to build our education on such things our structure is hardly worth the building; and second, that all children can be educated, some in one way, some in another, and it is our business to so shape our program that education should result from those things we bring to them. . . . We are pointing the way, we are creating the atmosphere that makes people willing to seek, that they may find. . . . So you and I . . . are engaged in the highest, and I believe, the holiest of all pieces of educational work. (*Journal of Proceedings of the Music Supervisors National Conference* 1929, 165–72)

A Code of Ethics

Shortly after World War II, AASA and the Music Educators National Conference cooperated with the American Federation of Musicians on a common problem. Many school performing groups had become very proficient and were often exploited for commercial purposes. Band directors and their students felt complimented when they were asked to provide the music for the opening of new commercial ventures or to entertain at professional athletic events. But professional musicians resented their own children being asked to take work away from them. School administrators pointed out that their students' musical experiences often did not justify the time away from school. In 1947, James C. Petrillo, president of the American Federation of Musicians, Luther A. Richman, president of the Music Educators National Conference, and Harold C. Hunt of the American Association of School Administrators agreed on a code of ethics (American Federation of Musicians 1947).

The *Code of Ethics* clarified the kinds of events for which school organizations and professional musicians could provide music. Students could play for school and civic events, educational broadcasts, and benefit performances for charities and not-for-profit and noncommercial enterprises. Professional musicians could play for entertainment, including athletic events, festivals, and celebrations. *The Code of Ethics* has been renewed many times since it was created and it continues to protect students against exploitation.

In 1959, the American Association of School Administrators spoke for school music again. After the Soviet Union launched Sputnik in 1957 and became the first country to orbit a satellite, there was intense pressure to increase mathematics and science requirements. Some school systems upset the curriculum balance in favor of those subjects. The problem was called to the attention of AASA by Vannet Lawler, executive secretary of the Music Educators National Conference, and the AASA planned its 1959 convention on a creative arts theme. Again, excellent school music groups performed, and this time poets, artists, and dancers were part of the program. Joseph Maddy, founder of the National Music Camp and MENC president from 1938 to 1939, received the prestigious American Education Award. The meeting and the resolution it produced improved the climate for arts education significantly.

The AASA assisted MENC once more in the 1970s by passing a resolution: "When cuts in the curriculum become necessary, they should be made across the board rather than categorically."

The National Society for the Study of Education (NSSE)

At the meeting of the National Education Association in 1895, a group of educators interested in the serious study of education formed the National Herbart Society, named in honor of the German philosopher Johann Friedrich Herbart's contribution to the science of education. Music education was not a central topic of discussion for some time, although it was often mentioned in association with other topics. The name of the organization was changed to the National Society for the Study of Education (NSSE) in 1901. Its 1936 annual report was about music education. It included papers written by several music education leaders, and the profession gained prestige from having been highlighted by this elite organization. In 1958, NSSE focused on music education again. Thurber Madison of Indiana University headed another distinguished group to prepare *Basic Concepts in Music Education*. This landmark publication is discussed later.

The National Association of Secondary School Principals (NASSP)

The National Association of Secondary School Principals was founded in 1916, and several issues of the NASSP *Bulletin* have been devoted to music education. They include issues entitled "The Function of Music in the Secondary Schools" (November 1952), "Music—A Vital Force in To-day's Secondary Schools" (March 1959), and "Music Education: Its Place in Secondary Schools" (October 1975). "The Arts in the Comprehensive High School" was another influential issue of the *Bulletin* prepared by a committee of NASSP.

The NASSP Contest and Activities Committee has provided guidance to music educators by evaluating various events across the country and approving the ones considered beneficial to students and to education. MENC and NASSP worked with the North Central Association of Colleges and Secondary Schools in preparing and disseminating "Guiding Principles for School Music Group Activities."

The National Association of Elementary School Principals (NAESP)

NAESP was founded in 1920, and has provided a forum for music educators to promote music for younger school children. NAESP members have written articles for the *National Elementary School Principal*, appeared on NAESP convention programs, and served on joint committees of MENC and NAESP. The February 1951 and December 1959 issues of *The Principal* were devoted entirely to music. MENC reproduced the issues for distribution to its own members.

Accrediting Agencies

The National Association of Schools of Music (NASM) was created in 1924 to accredit all music degree programs. For some time thereafter, music teacher training programs were approved both by NASM and the various state accrediting offices. Public school music leaders provided guidance to NASM, which was controlled at first by conservatory people oriented toward European music. The growth of school music programs created a demand for licensed music teachers, which in turn increased the size of college faculties, making stronger programs possible. This made some of the great music schools of the nation viable, especially at state universities.

In 1952, the American Association of Colleges of Teacher Education, which had begun its own accreditation process in 1927, joined with the Council of Chief State School Officers, the National Association of State

Directors of Teacher Education and Certification, the National School Boards Association, and the NEA Commission on Teacher Education and Professional Standards to form the National Council for the Accreditation of Teacher Education. In 1970, the organization was named the "sole agency for the accreditation of teachers, educational administrators and school service personnel" by the National Commission on Accrediting. NASM has continued to accredit music education programs of its member institutions.

The Music Educators National Conference

Philip Hayden was the primary figure in the founding of the Music Supervisors National Conference (later Music Educators National Conference). The organization began with an invitation by Hayden to music supervisors to meet in Keokuk, Iowa. The 1906 meeting of the National Education Association had been cancelled because of the San Francisco earthquake, and a meeting was scheduled for 1907 in Los Angeles instead. Hayden expected few Midwestern music supervisors to attend the west coast meeting. Although he supported the NEA Department of Music Education and promoted its meetings in the magazine he founded in 1900, *School Music Monthly*, he criticized the NEA meetings. He described them as "disconnected conventions, each almost wholly independent of those preceding and following, without any relation to a consistent and abiding aim" *(School Music* 1904, 8). In the November 1904 issue of *School Music,* Hayden called the NEA meetings "too barren of features . . . to travel half-way across the United States to hear six or eight papers which, a little later, they could read in their own homes" (10).

Haydn was an alumnus of New York University and Oberlin College and was a part-time reporter for the *Quincy* (Illinois) *Daily Journal.* He had run his own music studio in Quincy before a school supervisory position was created for him. *School Music Monthly* succeeded because of his careful and meticulous planning, although it was never actually issued every month. It merged with Helen Place's *Journal of School Music* in 1903 and continued as *School Music* until publication ceased in 1936.

The Call to Keokuk

After the 1906 NEA meeting was canceled, Haydn wrote to 30 Midwestern music supervisors on November 27, 1906, inviting them to Keokuk to observe his work in school-music rhythm. He proposed that the

Figure 3.1. *School Music Monthly* cover.

convention last "two days, comprising six lessons with a regular program, my work in ear training in rhythm forms to take up two or three of these sessions, the rest of the meeting to be given up to problems of general interest, to papers and discussions" (Channon 1959, 62). Edward Bailey Birge, who helped Hayden with the final program, wrote that his friend was careful to avoid undermining the NEA and was not proposing a national affair (Birge 1966, 241; *School Music* 1908, 20).

The Keokuk Meeting

To Haydn's surprise, 104 supervisors from fourteen states accepted his invitation, some from as far away as New York, Washington, DC, and Texas. Keokuk, a city of 16,000 in southeast Iowa, was well-prepared to host the event. It had seven hotels and twenty-seven boarding houses at that time (*McCoy's Keokuk City Directory* 2007, 282). The Grand Theater was made available and the Monday Music Club pitched in to help with administrative and logistical tasks. The first order of business was the appointment of an auditing committee, which assessed all of the attendees seventy-five cents,[1] probably to cover the meals they had together, the costs of the opera, and other expenses. After that, papers and musical performances were presented. The Keokuk Board of Education voted to close the city's eleven schools at 10:30 on Friday, the final day of the conference, so classroom teachers could attend the events.

On the last day, Friday, there was a performance in the Grand Theater of Jesse Gaynor's children's operetta, *The House that Jack Built,* featuring 150 children and fifty adults. The lead roles were sung by members of the Keokuk local opera company. The conference closed on Friday evening with a meal prepared and served by the ladies of the Westminster Presbyterian Church.

About one-third of the meeting was dedicated to Hayden's rhythm form demonstrations, and the format had features that continued in later meetings (Molnar 1955, 42). Papers were presented, and local school children took part in demonstrations of teaching strategies. Alys Bentley, of Washington, DC, had a group of first graders imitate the sounds of nature as preparation for singing in the opening sessions. Girls glee clubs from Keokuk and Carthage High Schools sang during afternoon breaks. Musical presentations by students were an important part of the meeting (*Keokuk Daily Gate City* 1907, 1). The attendees also made music themselves, as they still do at conventions.

---

1. Seventy-five cents in 1907 was the equivalent of about $16 in 2008.

When the supervisors came together for the Cincinnati meeting in 1910, they adopted a constitution and their organization officially became the Music Supervisors National Conference (MSNC). The attendees declared two purposes: mutual helpfulness and the promotion of good music through the instrumentality of the public schools. Hayden finally had the independent professional organization he had worked for. From the beginning, publishers and other suppliers offered financial support. C. C. Birchard had been closely associated with school music since the early days of the summer schools that were sponsored by book companies and had strongly favored an independent professional association. MSNC appeared at a time when the country was expanding, its industrial base was growing, and millions of immigrants were pouring in. The creation of a national organization to serve the nation's cultural needs at that particular time was fortuitous.

By 1918, the MSNC's Educational Council was created because the membership was too large for decisions to be made by individual vote. The council was charged with establishing direction and priorities beyond the particular interests of the presidents, who served only a one-year term at that time. Will Earhart was appointed chairman. Other council members were Hollis Dann, Peter W. Dykema, Charles H. Farnsworth, Karl W. Gehrkens, Thaddeus P. Giddings, Alice Inskeep, Osbourn McConathy, W. Otto Miessner, and Charles H. Miller..

Karl Gehrkens and Hollis Dann were assigned the task of making recommendations for a collegiate course of study to prepare supervisors. Their report was accepted on April 8, 1921, and was published, together with *The Standard Course in Music for the Elementary Grades,* as *Bulletin No. 1.* The Educational Council's report contained a statement that prepared the way for action taken by school administrators in 1927:

> Music has proven itself worthy to be classed as a major subject, co-ordinate with reading, writing and arithmetic, and must no longer be considered an adjunct more or less superfluous and unrelated to educational processes. Therefore the music supervisors voice the demand of musicians, music teachers, musical organizations and intelligent lovers of music as well as the progressive educators of the country for such readjustment of the school curriculum as will make possible the proper and adequate teaching and use of music as an integral part of the regular school work.

Bulletin No. 1 was the first of a series of publications on numerous topics that have reappeared in many publications, conferences, and other forums since that time. It cost ten cents during the early years. The titles of the first three *Bulletins* indicate how MSNC served its membership and the profession:

1921   No. 1: *Standard Course in Music for the Elementary Grades and Four-Year Course for Training Music Supervisors*
1922   No. 2: *High School Credits for Applied Music Study*
        No. 3: *Report on the Study of Music Instruction in the Public Schools of the U.S.*
1925   No. 4: *Junior High School Music*
        No. 5: *Standard Course of Training in Music for Grade Teachers*
        No. 6: *High School Credits for Applied Music Study*
        No. 7: *Report on the Study of Music Instruction*
        No. 8: *Junior High School Music*
1926   No. 9: *Report on Music in the One-Teacher Rural School*
        No. 10: *Survey on Tests and Measurements in Music Education*
        No. 11: *College Entrance Credits and College Course in Music*
        No. 12: *Standards of Attainment for Sight-Singing at the End of the Sixth Grade*
        No. 13: *High School Music Credit Course*
        No. 14: *The Accrediting of Music Teachers*
        No. 15: *Contests, Competitions and Festival Meets*
        No. 16: *Newer Practices and Tendencies in Music Education*

Music for Every Child, Every Child for Music

Willis P. Kent, a teacher at the Ethical Culture School in New York, gave a speech entitled "Music for Every Man" at the meeting in Pittsburgh in 1915. The next year, Peter W. Dykema, Kent's former colleague at the New York school, spoke about community music to the American Academy of Political and Social Science. He used the phrase, "music for the people, music by the people, and music of the people." He was relating music education to the future of the nation. When Osbourne McConathy was planning the 1919 meeting in Saint Louis, he announced his theme: "Every child should be educated in music in accordance with his capacities, at public expense and his musical development should function in the life of the community." Later, he wrote:

> I have twisted and turned this statement in innumerable ways in an endeavor to abbreviate it until it might serve as slogan, but all my efforts in this direction have been unavailing. I have not been able to find

words with which to state the proposition more briefly. (McConathy 1919, 24–25)

Otto Miessner picked up on the idea in a speech entitled *Music Democratized*: "What is the place for music in the new educational democracy?" He argued that the supervisors had too narrow a vision, and he made a plea "to democratize music by teaching it in all branches, instrumental as well as vocal, in classes like other subjects and at public expense. Let us give music, the best we have, to all of the people (*Music Supervisors Journal* September 1919, 10). Miessner urged that children be treated as individuals and not be forced to sing if they showed an aptitude for instrumental music. This was consonant with the Progressive Education Association, which was organized that year.

A Standard Course of Study

The first task of the MSNC's Educational Council was the creation of a standard course of study for the first six grades by 1919. From the beginning of school music, the subject matter taught in the schools had been determined by the particular book adopted for the class and the method that was associated with it. At the 1921 meeting, the Council reported on the standards it had agreed upon. They were described in terms of competencies, a concept that was ahead of its time.

The 1922 conference was held in Nashville, Tennessee. President Frank Beach's belief was similar to Osborne McConathy's, who said in 1919: "Every boy and every girl in every section of our country has the right to efficient daily instruction in music in the public schools." The slogan was too long, so Beach shortened it to "More Music in Education: More Education in Music." Thirteen years later, the slogan that McConathy had searched for earlier suddenly came to him—"Music for Every Child, Every Child for Music." The motto expressed the democratic feeling that so many had been speaking and writing about for years. Gehrkens made it the theme for his meeting and MSNC has used it in many ways since 1923.

Publications

At the Minneapolis meeting in 1914, there was a discussion of how to extend MSNC's influence. Giddings suggested that, instead of publishing an annual book of proceedings, MSNC should consider issuing it in four installments to every supervisor at no charge. Frances Elliott Clark spoke against the idea because a yearbook was essential to the organization. The

Board of Directors compromised and agreed to publish a journal that would be sent free to supervisors, but would not replace the *Proceedings*.

Peter W. Dykema was appointed editor of *The Music Supervisors Bulletin*. It was an expensive undertaking for a young organization whose annual membership dues were only one dollar after paying two dollars for the initial year of membership, but publishers' advertisements helped support it. It was published four times a year and sent free to all interested in school music. With the September 1915 issue, the name of the periodical was changed to *Music Supervisors Journal*. In that issue, C. A. Farnsworth recommended that a permanent editor be hired in view of the rapid expansion the conference was undergoing (*Music Supervisors Journal* 2 September 1915, 10). No action was taken by the Board of Directors, and the *Journal* and the *Proceedings* continued to be prepared *gratis* by appointed members for another fifteen years.

The volunteer efforts of the editors made valuable contributions to the professionalism of the organization. This is especially true of Peter Dykema. His name is one of the most revered in the history of the Music Educators National Conference. One of his many contributions was the promotion of community singing. Dykema suggested that MSNC should promote singing by selecting a small number of songs that teachers could concentrate their attention on. He was appointed head of a committee of three charged with the responsibility of developing a list of not more than twelve songs appropriate for group singing. Ultimately, eighteen songs were chosen and published in 1913 in a pamphlet produced by the Birchard Publishing Company. It sold for five cents, or four dollars a hundred.[2] Dykema's performance in his first assignment was impressive, and he was appointed second vice president with the responsibility of editing the magazine. He later reminisced that the board did not hamper the editor "with any funds for carrying on the work," but he produced four issues and mailed out a total of 25,000 copies with the help of the book publishers. He ended the year with a balance of less than $100, which MSNC used for the publication of the *Proceedings*. Dykema's dedication to MSNC and his strong faith in music led him to value community singing as an important undertaking. He published reports of promotional ideas and successful community sings in various parts of the country in a feature Dykema called "For Your Local Papers." In 1917, the Community Music Committee expanded the number of songs from eighteen to fifty-five.

---

2. The songs were "America," "Star Spangled Banner," "Come Thou Almighty King," "Swanee River," "O How Lovely Is the Evening," "The Ash Grove," "*Auld Lang Syne*," "Dixie," "Annie Laurie," "My Old Kentucky Home," "How Can I Leave Thee," "Flow Gently Sweet Afton," "O *Tannenbaum*" (translated), "Nancy Lee," "O Who Will O'er the Downs," "Minstrel Boy," "A Capital Ship," and "Row, Row, Row the Boat."

The *Liberty Edition* was released when the United States entered World War I in 1917, and soon after, the *Twice 55* series. Other publishers produced their own collections. Hall and McCreary's *Golden Book of Favorite Songs* was one of the most popular. Community sings flourished across the country. Birchard made the Committee's *55 Songs and Choruses* available just before the 1917 meeting in Grand Rapids. Dykema wrote in the *Music Supervisors Journal*: "Every time the book is used, the claims of public school music from which the book arose are strengthened. As the people sing more they appreciate better the claims of music for a larger place in our educational system."

Just in time for the declaration of war against Germany, *55 Songs* appeared in April and patriotic rallies became even more popular. Thanks to MSNC, the country was prepared to sing the national, traditional, and patriotic songs as well as George M. Cohan's and Irving Berlin's songs that stirred Americans.[3] Dykema published Hamlin Cogswell's account of conducting thirty-two thousand citizens in a carol sing in front of the Treasury Building in Washington, DC, just before Christmas in 1917. Some music educators disagreed with using popular music in community sings. They thought of the sings as a way to make America serious about what they considered good music, which did not include popular songs. Dykema recognized the value of some popular music. He published letters from song leaders John Beattie and Duncan McKenzie. They praised the music their colleagues considered trivial because they had seen what popular songs could do for the spirits of the men in uniform (*Music Supervisors Journal* 5 September 1918, 5).

Community singing was an important part of the World War I effort. It helped keep morale high in the military, and many musicians were trained to be military song leaders. Maxwell Bartholomew and Robert Lawrence wrote:

> Aided by the splendid spirit of patriotism which swept the country after the declaration of war, and realizing the great need of music to help build morale, wonders were accomplished in incredibly short periods of time. . . . A proof of the popularity of this singing program may be found in the fact that in the contonments [*sic*] of the United States during the second year of the war (1918), there was an attendance of thirty-seven millions at soldier gatherings in Y.M.C.A. huts at which the main attraction, frequently the only one, was mass singing. More than thirty thousand soldier song leaders were trained. Everywhere the army went they sang. The result in fighting spirit has been testified to by military leaders the country over. (Bartholomew and Lawrence 1920, 16–17)

---

3. For example, "You're a Grand Old Flag," "Over There," "I'll Be Home for Christmas," and "God Bless America."

Figure 3.2A.   Class of YMCA song leaders being trained at Camp Kearny, California (position of "cut-off"). B. Song leader candidates under instruction at Northwestern University (position of rhythmic hold). From Marshall Bartholomew and Robert Lawrence, *Music for Everybody: Organization and Leadership of Community Music Activities* **(New York: Abingdon Press, 1920).**

Together, the War Camp Community Service, the Commission on Training Camp Activities, and the YMCA hired excellent professional song leaders, and many hundreds of volunteers gave similar service independently throughout the country. Trained song leaders were sent into the war industry factories where workers were encouraged to sing at noon hours and during rest periods.

Frances Elliott Clark reflected that the action in Rochester in 1913 was taken because the route to making America musical through the schools was too slow. The supervisors wanted to share the joy of experiencing uplifting song by offering singing opportunities to all adults in their communities. The community music movement served the country and it helped MSNC gain acceptance as a force in American education.

"The Star Spangled Banner"

One and a half million copies of *55 Songs* were sold in the first eighteen months, and the new *Liberty Edition* was released in the summer of 1918. It had more patriotic songs and a new, more singable version of the national anthem. The supervisors working on the new version learned that another group was doing the same thing for the *Army Songbook*. Commercial publishers were undecided about which version to print, and so a joint committee created the service version. Clifford V. Buttelman, the first executive secretary of MSNC, described the organization's involvement in the project in a pamphlet titled "The Music Supervisors National Conference and the Star Spangled Banner."

The Great Immigration

Community spirit and wartime patriotism were not the only reasons for MSNC to promote community singing. A huge influx of people from the poorer countries of Europe, especially Eastern Europe, came to the United States during the period known as the Great Immigration (c. 1880–1920). They came to America to escape poverty and political and religious persecution. Most of these new Americans did not speak English and were different in many other ways from their established countrymen. Americans believed their country to be a melting pot,[4] where new Americans were acculturated through societal institutions (the schools, the workplace, the streets, the military, civic organizations) to speak, act, and think like established Americans. The schools were one of the tools that helped acculturate new Americans to their unfamiliar surroundings, and music was an important part of the process.

George Oscar Bowen, head of the University of Michigan Department of Public School Music, succeeded Dykema as editor in 1921 and was the first national president to organize a biennial convention and the first to

---

4. So called after the name of the popular play, *The Melting Pot*, by Israel Zangwill in 1907.

hold office for a two-year period. The centerpiece of his convention was the first national high school chorus, directed by Hollis Dann. The Flint (Michigan) High School A Cappella Choir began an era of unaccompanied singing in American schools (Kegerris 1966, 254–65).

REGIONAL ORGANIZATIONS

A few delegates from the eastern states and some members from the Boston Pulse Club laid the groundwork for the first of the regional divisions on the train trip from the Grand Rapids convention in 1917. Frederick Archibald of Waltham, Massachusetts, and Howard Davis of Chelsea, Massachusetts, planned organizational meetings and in May 1918 four hundred eastern music supervisors met in Boston. There was concern that the new organization would separate from MSNC, but the leaders of both the national and regional organizations believed that the regional needed to be subordinate.

The Southern Division began when the southern supervisors asked MSNC to hold its national meeting in Nashville in 1922. There, more than one hundred Southerners formed the Southern Music Supervisors Conference, and Paul Weaver was elected president. The Southern group dropped the word *supervisor* from its title when it adopted the name Southern Conference for Music Education.

Mabelle Glenn was elected president of the Southwestern Division, and she planned its first meeting in Tulsa. Oklahoma, Arkansas, and Texas were divorced from the Southern Division, and with Colorado, Kansas, Missouri, and New Mexico, made up the balance of the Southwestern Division.

The North Central division elected Anton Embs of Oak Park, Illinois, president. It met in Springfield, Illinois, a central location in the vast expanse of the ten states that stretch from the Dakotas to the Ohio River and from the North Platte in Nebraska to the shores of Lake Huron in Michigan.

After a meeting of the National Education Association in Seattle in 1927, several music supervisors formed the Northwest Division. Its first conference was held in Spokane in 1929 with Letha McClure, director of music in Seattle, as president.

What is now the Western Division began as the California Division. It became the California-Western Division when it incorporated four states, with Utah having been transferred from the Southwestern Division. The first meeting was held in Los Angeles in 1931 with Herman Trutner as president. The Western Division eventually included Hawaii and Guam.

The Music Supervisors Journal

Paul Weaver, the editor of the *Music Supervisors Journal,* could not get a second-class mailing privilege because the journal did not have paying subscribers. In his last issue as editor (May 1930), he announced that with the establishment of the headquarters office, subscriptions would be one dollar for nonmembers, which would be allocated to the magazine. That would create the paid list required by the United States Postal Service for the second-class privilege. It was granted in 1930.

Under the journal's new organizational scheme, Executive Secretary Clifford V. Buttelman was to be the managing editor and Edward Bailey Birge the chairman of the editorial board. Vanett Lawler, the first employee hired by Buttelman, was gifted in working with the music industry, and the magazine thrived. When MSNC changed its name to Music Educators National Conference in 1934, the periodical followed suit and became the *Music Educators Journal.* The MENC board of directors named Birge chairman emeritus in appreciation for his contributions to the magazine and the organization. His close friend and associate, Will Earhart, wrote: "His dry wit, his sometimes acid humor, his never failing crusade for brevity and crispness not only have made working with him a delight, but have borne fruit in establishing sound editorial standards for the *Journal*" (Earhart 1944, 13, 59). Birge is also remembered for writing the first history of American music education, published by the Oliver Ditson Company. The publisher gave the rights to the book to MENC in 1966.

President Russell Morgan found ways to expand opportunities for any member who wanted to contribute services for the good of the profession. In a letter to a colleague written in 1930 he wrote: "The total power of our group is enhanced by the growth of the individuals who wholeheartedly or even causally take part in . . . cooperative assignments and projects, even though nothing ever appears in print to record their efforts and contributions" (Buttelman 1955, xi). Much has appeared in print as the result of the voluntary work of the membership since that time. The list of bulletins continued to increase rapidly. Seven revisions of *Bulletin No. 17* (*Music Buildings, Rooms, and Equipment*) appeared until 1987. This bulletin was used by architects throughout the country to design excellent music facilities.

MSNC Headquarters

Music education had just completed a decade of growth during which instrumental music was added to the curriculum. Membership increased significantly during that time. The phenomenal success of Joseph Maddy's National High School Orchestra at the 1927 meeting of the Department of Superintendence stimulated the superintendents to call for music to be given equal consideration with other subjects in the high schools. The time had come for MSNC to have an office and a permanent staff to carry on its business. The office was opened in the Lyon & Healy Building in Suite 820, 64 East Jackson Boulevard in Chicago in 1930, shortly after the October 1929 Wall Street crash. Buttelman made a good choice when he hired Vanett Lawler as his first employee. They worked together as a team for twenty-six years, and when she succeeded Buttelman as executive secretary, he continued on for a few years to produce the *Journal*.

The Great Depression of the 1930s affected the headquarters office, as it did every school system. Local merchants had to carry the employees "on the tab" when there were no funds to pay the staff until the membership dues arrived. It even became necessary for MENC to reduce its budget by lending Lawler to the Pan-American Union in Washington. She worked closely with Charles Seeger, the distinguished musicologist, composer, and folklorist in Washington. Seeger broadened her view of music and society, which helped prepare her to lead MSNC. She made several trips to Latin America to teach music educators how to organize associations that could improve music education in their schools. Her Washington experience also gave her the chance to help MENC move to the National Education Association Center in Washington.

The first two executive secretaries built a structure for the national organization, including a federated unit in each state, auxiliary organizations that included the Music Exhibitors Association (created in 1926), and a collection of associated groups that represented MSNC special interest members. The new office managed the *Journal* and ran the national and divisional meetings on a more businesslike basis. The recently established Music Exhibitors Association arranged displays of instruments and music, and the office staff planned for the exhibits, advertised the space, and sold the display booths. The displays became an increasingly important part of the meetings that contributed financially to the organization. The permanent executive staff provided continuity to the organization. The team of Buttelman and Lawler, with helpers like Helen Peterson, Helen Hatter, and Edna Pierce, soon became expert at handling all of the meeting responsibilities. Buttelman later referred to himself as an "organization engineer."

The 1940 Constitution

The Music Supervisors National Conference changed its name to Music Educators National Conference (MENC) in 1934 because its members had become music teachers who no longer supervised classroom teachers. When MENC adopted a new constitution in 1940, it became a department of NEA and it absorbed the fifty-six-year-old NEA Department of Music Education.

The new constitution made it clear that there was one organization with a central headquarters. It was one conference, operating a biennial national meeting with six alternate year national meetings in the geographical divisions (Grant 1940, 462–64). All meetings, and even the makeup of the divisions, were under the jurisdiction of the national board of directors. The constitution also made clear that the affiliated state units were an important part of the structure.

The concept of a totally unified organization working at national, divisional, and state levels was the most critical element, and the state units were enhanced by being part of a national organization. The first state organizations grew from associations of instrumental music teachers who needed to solve problems associated with statewide contests and festivals. A unified state and national dues structure helped many state units because unification required all members to pay dues to a state organization. The state units developed local activities that attracted members who could not take their groups to state-sponsored events without at least partial membership in the national organization. This category of membership required full membership in the state organization and a subscription to the *Music Educators Journal*. That membership category was created to build state units and a fully unified national organization. By the end of 1940 there were nineteen state units. World War II slowed the process, but by April 1945, the number of fully affiliated state organizations had grown to thirty-two.

There was a problem with the Texas unit. The majority of Texas band directors refused to pay even partial membership dues to MENC, and when MENC eliminated its partial membership category in 1958, that made it even more difficult to persuade them to join. The problem was solved when a new organization, the Texas Music Educators Conference, was founded. It replaced the Texas Music Educators Association as an MENC affiliate.

In 1940, MENC published an important pamphlet entitled "Outline of a Program for Music Education." Five basic music activities—singing, rhythmics, listening, playing, and creating—were recommended for the elementary school. The minimum daily amounts of time suggested for music at the various levels were twenty minutes for kindergarten through third grade and twenty-five to thirty minutes for grades 4 through 6. It recommended five types of activities that should be offered at the junior high school level and for grades 10, 11, and 12. The pamphlet recommended assembly programs, concerts, and recitals by student performers, educational concerts, music clubs, and community music programs.

The outline suggested a model for school systems by which music programs could be measured. Music educators posted them on school bulletin boards and used the recommendations to strengthen their programs. Conference sessions were keyed to the outline. The outline brought some stability to music education because it symbolized nationwide agreement on music instruction and helped create some uniformity in the profession. It was updated in 1951 and continued to be used for many years.

1940 Yearbook

The yearbooks that MENC published from 1910 to 1940 illustrate how complex music education had become in thirty years. The substantive portion of the 1940 yearbook encompassed 460 pages in eight sections:

    I. Music in Education and Life (philosophy and sociology)
    II. Special Phases and Applications (research)
    III. Current Trends in Music Education (curriculum and regional problems)
    IV. Instrumental Music
    V. Piano Class Instruction
    VI. Vocal Music
    VII. Music in Colleges and Universities
    VIII. Teacher Training

Another 150 pages covered indices and "Organizational Miscellany." The yearbook illustrated the size and complexity of MENC at the age of thirty-three.

In-and-About Clubs

American society in the first half of the twentieth century was becoming increasingly urbanized. Concentrations of schools usually meant there were many music educators within a short distance of each other, although they could still feel isolated because there was usually only one in each school. After World War I, MSNC members in metropolitan areas began to meet in what became known as in-and-about clubs. Before state associations were established, these clubs were a vehicle for sharing professional ideas and for social contact among music educators. Meetings were usually held in central locations, often restaurants. Thirty-one in-and-about clubs existed in 1940, but the number dropped rapidly after World War II as the state associations became more active.

Rural Schools

There were outstanding music education programs before World War II in the large city school systems and in some small towns, but the profession was concerned about children in one- or two-room schoolhouses. The *Research Council Bulletin* #6 (1926) sparked interest in rural music education. In the next few years, supervisory positions that included rural music education were created in Louisiana, Virginia, Missouri, California, and Montana. Marguerite Hood was persistent and innovative in bringing music to students in Montana's one-room rural schools. She began a series of music education broadcasts in 1936 in violation of a policy of the American Society of Recording Artists (ASRA) that required radio stations to pay royalties for recordings they played on air. She appealed to the singer Al Jolson to support her cause because of his star-status as a recording artist. Jolson agreed and addressed the ASRA board of directors. Shortly after, Arthur W. Levy, ASRA executive secretary, informed Hood that the Society would not interfere with her important broadcasts to Montana's children. She became radio director for the KGVO *Montana School of the Air* program, and later was an announcer, writer, and reporter for three CBS local stations (Cooper 2005, 296–97).

Samuel Burns, Lloyd Funchess, Charles Fullerton, and Luther Richman also supported rural music education. More than 4,000 rural children from Missouri sang at the 1938 MENC convention to demonstrate the success of the state's first year of experience with a statewide program. Nine states had appointed supervisors of music by 1939 and seventeen other state directors of education recognized the need for them. In the 1952–1953 school year there were still more than 45,000 one-room schools and over 11,000 two-room schools in operation. Increased consolidation, more states with state supervisors of music, radios, phonographs, and better texts improved the situation in most sections of the country, but instrumental music instruction for all children in smaller schools still needed special attention (Annett 1955, 83–85).

MENC and World War II

MENC leaders Louis Woodson Curtis, Fowler Smith, and Lilla Belle Pitts all worked closely with Executive Secretary Buttelman to provide the support of MENC for all aspects of the war effort. Music educators were encouraged by President Franklin D. Roosevelt's call for "more bands, more parades, more flag waving" to build national spirit. The board of directors adopted a wartime theme in 1940: "American Unity through Music."

MENC participated in the war effort by conducting classes for training community song leaders and coordinating efforts for the Civilian Defense Organization, the Policies Commission of the National Education Association, the U.S. Army Morale Division, and the National Recreation Association. Patriotic song lists were prepared, as in World War I (Mark 1980, 34). As Congress was passing the Lend Lease Law in early 1941, MENC was preparing an eight-page section for the March-April issue of the *Music Educators Journal* that emphasized "Music in Our Democracy." It listed four areas for attention by music educators: singing national songs, developing respect for music of the various heritages and races in the United States, singing folk and pioneer songs, and giving attention to the music of American composers. There was also a Latin American component labeled "Music for Uniting the Americas," intended to familiarize music educators with musics of South America and Central America, and making North American music available to music educators in Latin countries. Harold Spivacke of the music division of the Library of Congress helped select folk songs for use in schools, and the newly established music division of the Pan American Union prepared lists of songs.

Another article in *Music Educators Journal* titled "Music as a Restorative Force," announced that "our institutions, our very way of life, our form of government are being attacked by organized propaganda." Howard Hanson of the Eastman School of Music warned:

> As we go into the program of national defense which is occupying so much of our thought, we must see to it that the emphasis upon material defense does not leave us spiritually bankrupt. . . . We must fight the good fight against materialism to the end that the world not be deprived of beauty. In saving our bodies we must not lose our souls.

The war made changes that affected music programs. Schedules changed from the seven- or eight-period school day to five or six periods to allow students to do their homework during the longer periods. That saved electricity in the evenings. Many school systems neglected to change back after the war, and many students found it impossible to schedule choir or orchestra.

There were inconveniences during the war. The government put an excise tax on musical instruments, as it did on many other items. Instruments were hard to purchase in any event, as the military organizations took almost everything the industry could produce. Travel restrictions eliminated the regional and national competitive events, and contests beyond state boundaries have not had the sanction of MENC since that time.

Community music became important again. Augustus Zanzig, music consultant to the Treasury Department, was a workshop leader at the 1943 division meetings, which were billed as "Institutes on Music Education in Wartime." The Radio Branch of the Bureau of Public Relations of the War Department prepared a brochure entitled "Music in the National War Effort." The 100,000 copies allocated to MENC quickly ran out. Marshall Bartholomew, the director of the Yale Glee Club, who had been trapped in Europe by World War I when he was a student of Englebert Humperdinck, wrote a piece for the *Journal* in which he told his colleagues, "Our job is to blow the trumpet, beat the drum and keep singing."

MENC continued to hold its divisional and national conventions during the early part of the war, but the six 1945 divisional meetings were cancelled and the scheduled elections were conducted by mail. The Office of Defense Transportation had set limits on attendance at meetings that required extensive travel, and only fifty members from each division were allowed to attend what became known as the "Six-Fifties."

The end of the war in 1945 brought profound societal changes, especially in higher education. The percentage of the population enrolled in schools had declined, especially at the secondary level. The G.I. Bill, however, created a new surge of college enrollment. Many veterans eligible for education assistance under the G.I. Bill pursued graduate degrees, and enrollments in university music education programs increased dramatically. MENC produced its "Outline of the Course in Music Education Leading to the Master's Degree."

The Journal of Research in Music Education

There were increased research expectations, and many master's degree programs required students to write a thesis. Doctoral programs carried research further, and the numbers of serious scholars began to increase. As new graduate programs in music education increased, it became apparent to university music educators that a journal was needed to report research results. During a visit to Marguerite Hood at the University of Michigan during her MENC presidency, Warren Freeman, dean of the Boston University School of Music, suggested that MENC should provide a scholarly outlet (Britton 1984, 233). Allen P. Britton, a member of the University of Michigan faculty, participated in the discussion. He submitted a proposal to the MENC board of directors that was accepted in 1952.

Britton was the founding editor. He published the first issue in 1953, and by its twentieth anniversary it had become a prominent scholarly journal, with a circulation exceeding 4,000. The *Journal of Research in Music Education* created the opportunity for a community of music education scholars to develop. By the early 1960s, that community was established and contributing valuable information to the music education profession.

A significant event in music education research of the 1990s was the publication of the *Handbook of Research on Music Teaching and Learning* in 1992. Edited by Richard Colwell, the handbook contained fifty-five chapters written by more than seventy scholars and researchers (Colwell 1992). The second volume, *The New Handbook of Research on Music Teaching and Learning*, was published in 2002. Colwell and Carol Richardson were the editors.

Interest in qualitative research grew throughout the 1990s. The journal *Update: Applications of Research in Music Education* was added to the list of periodicals published by MENC (after having been issued for several years by the University of South Carolina). *Update* bridges the gap between researchers and practitioners.

Other Research Activities

The expanded interest in research stimulated initiatives outside of MENC. The Council for Research in Music Education (CRME) was founded in 1963 by the University of Illinois and the Illinois Office of the Superintendent of Public Instruction. The CRME *Bulletin* is published by The University of Illinois. CRME also publishes indices of music education doctoral dissertations in progress and of recently completed dissertations.

Other music education research journals include *The Missouri Journal of Research in Music Education* (Missouri State Department of Education, founded 1962), *The Bulletin of Research* (Pennsylvania Music Educators Association, founded 1963), *Contributions to Music Education* (Ohio Music Educators Association, founded 1972), *The Bulletin of Historical Research in*

Music Education (founded in 1980 at the University of Kansas, later relocated to Ithaca College), and *Update: The Applications of Research in Music Education* (University of South Carolina, founded 1982). In 1988 *Update* became an MENC publication. Volume I, no. 1, of the *Southeastern Journal of Music Education* was published in 1989 by the University of Georgia.

Special Research Interest Groups

Special Research Interest Groups (SRIGS) were formed at the 1978 MENC convention. The SRIGS, governed by the MENC music education research council, serve music educators who share similar research interests. Some of the groups focused on creativity, learning and development, measurement and evaluation, affective response, history, philosophy, instructional strategies, perception, and early childhood. Each of the thirteen SRIGS publishes its own newsletters and sponsors sessions at the MENC national conventions.

Research Symposia

A variety of research symposia has been presented for the benefit of music education researchers. Funding from the Theodore Presser Foundation made possible a series of meetings at the University of Michigan known as the Ann Arbor Symposium. The Ann Arbor Symposium, co-sponsored by MENC and the University of Michigan, was held between 1978 and 1982. The symposium brought music educators together with leading psychologists and learning theorists.

The Wesleyan Symposium on the Application of Social Anthropology to the Teaching and Learning of Music, sponsored by MENC, Wesleyan University, and the Theodore Presser Foundation, was held in 1984 to examine the relationship between social anthropology and music education. "One Hundred-Fifty Years of Music in American Schools" was a 1988 historical symposium at the University of Maryland College Park, sponsored by MENC and the University of Maryland in celebration of the sesquicentennial of music in American schools. It was the first major symposium dedicated to historical research in music education.

A Newly Stated Purpose for MENC

A constitutional revision was approved at the 1950 meeting to define the purpose of MENC as "the advancement of music education." After forty-three years, MENC became a voluntary education association whose activities were officially and legally for the benefit of society at large, rather than for its members. This was to become increasingly important as federal tax laws changed because it enabled the organization to take advantage of Internal Revenue 501(c)3 status, which protects not-for-profit organizations from expensive tax obligations.

Source Books

The materials developed by MENC commissions since 1942 were compiled in 1947 for the *Music Education Source Book* (1947), a compendium of writings about music education. The *Source Book* captured the essence of American music education in the 1940s. Eight years later another source book was published, this one entitled *Music in American Education,* also edited by Hazel Morgan.

Music in American Education was published in 1955, when MENC President Robert A. Choate had a new organizational scheme in place that he called "Music in American Life." Its ten commissions were:

Basic Concepts in Music Education
Standards of Musical Literature and Performance
Music in General School Administration
Music in Preschool, Kindergarten, Elementary School
Music in Junior High School
Music in Senior High School
Music in Higher Education
Music in the Community
Music in Media of Mass Communication
Accreditation and Certification

In addition to the commissions, there were four standing committees that addressed music for exceptional children, music in international relations, and organ and piano instruction in the schools.

Basic Concepts in Music Education

Changing societal conditions in the 1950s created new issues for music education leaders. Thurber Madison, chairman of the Basic Concepts Commission, arranged to have the final report, *Basic Concepts in Music Education,* published as the National Society for the Study of Education 1958 yearbook. *Basic Concepts* was widely adopted as a text in graduate music education programs.

Vanett Lawler

Clifford Buttelman served as executive secretary until 1955, when he was succeeded by Vanett Lawler. Lawler had twenty-five years of experience with the organization and had been a consultant to the Pan American Union. She was acting head of the Arts and Letters Section of the United Nations Educational, Social, and Cultural Organization (UNESCO) in Paris for six months. Her travels in fourteen Latin American countries made her an authority on how American music education could be helpful to other nations. Her work at the Pan American Union and as liaison to NEA and federal agencies during the war had made her familiar with the education scene in the nation's capital.

MENC Moves to Washington

The National Education Association built an education center in Washington, DC, in the 1950s, and offered free space to its departments. Lawler's first task as executive secretary was to oversee the move from Chicago to Washington, where she was to build a new staff. Her thirteen years of leadership were productive for MENC and for education. The MENC membership grew rapidly and her careful financial management built reserves. Some of her achievements were the Creative Arts Convention of the American Association of School Administrators, the Contemporary Music Project, underwritten by the Ford Foundation, and the International Society for Music Education, which she helped establish.

The National Interscholastic Music Activities Commission (NIMAC)

NIMAC, an MENC auxiliary, represented the contest and festival movement. The National High School Band Association and the National High School Orchestra Association were created to administer the national contests before World War II. The National School Vocal Association joined them in 1936, and the three groups merged into what was referred to as the National School Band, Orchestra, and Choral Association (NS-BOVA). In 1952, these groups became the National Interscholastic Music Activities Commission, an auxiliary organization with a seat on the MENC board of directors. They continued to publish selected music lists for the state festivals, prepared adjudication forms, and in 1963 published the *NI-MAC Manual*, a guide for interschool music activity. NIMAC was dissolved in 1968 because interscholastic activity either had become in-state activities or was controlled by regional organizations like the North Central Association of Colleges and Secondary Schools.

Associated Organizations

By 1940, music education had evolved into a broad and complex field with many specialties. The first were the college band directors, who organized in 1938 as the MENC Committee on College Bands and became the College Band Directors National Conference in 1940. Nine years later, the name was changed to the College Band Directors National Association (CBDNA), and it became an MENC associated organization. An even more specialized group, the National Association of College Wind and Percussion Instructors became associated with MENC in 1954.

In 1959, the American String Teachers Association began a relationship with MENC that led to associated status. The following year, MENC assisted a group of choral teachers when they held a one-day meeting in conjunction with the Atlantic City MENC convention. From this grew the American Choral Directors Association. The National School Orchestra Association became associated the same year and the National Band Association in 1962. In 1988, there were nine associated organizations—those mentioned above plus the National Jazz Educators Association, the National Black Music Caucus, and the Organization of American Kodály Educators.

THE TANGLEWOOD SYMPOSIUM

Shortly after Louis Wersen was elected MENC president in 1966, Edwin E. Stein, dean of the School of Music of Boston University, called on him to discuss Boston University's summer program at the Tanglewood Music Center in western Massachusetts. He offered the summer facility for a cooperative project if it would benefit MENC. They thought of a symposium that would allow MENC to respond to the findings of the Yale Seminar, which many music educators believed were made unfairly by musicians who were unfamiliar with public school music. MENC, Boston University, and the Theodore Presser Foundation sponsored the symposium, and Robert Choate was director. Wersen wrote in the foreword to the interpretive report of the Tanglewood project:

Tanglewood represents the unique situation of an organization taking stock of itself and its place in society. With no prompting from without, with no requirement for self-study as periodically befalls certain other institutions such as school systems or governmental agencies, MENC arranged to have its leaders and a group of distinguished outsiders turn appraising eyes on itself and the profession it represents. Recognizing complacency as a real danger for a successful organization, those who planned the Tanglewood Symposium chose to ask "How can we better serve?" and "What do we need to do to make music education more useful to the American society of today and tomorrow?" (Murphy and Sullivan 1967, ii)

At the end of the symposium, Allen Britton, Arnold Broido, and Charles Gary authored the declaration that summarized the symposium and provided guiding principals for the music education profession in a time of change. The Tanglewood Declaration follows:

The intensive evaluation of the role of music in American society and education provided by the Tanglewood Symposium of philosophers, educators, scientists, labor leaders, philanthropists, social scientists, theologians, industrialists, representatives of government and foundations, music educators, and other musicians led to this declaration:

We believe that education must have as major goals the art of living, the building of personal identity, and nurturing creativity. Since the study of music can contribute much to these ends, WE NOW CALL FOR MUSIC TO BE PLACED IN THE CORE OF THE SCHOOL CURRICULUM.

The arts afford a continuity with the aesthetic tradition in man's history. Music and other fine arts, largely nonverbal in nature, reach close to the social, psychological, and physiological roots of man in his search for identity and self-realization.

Educators must accept the responsibility for developing opportunities which meet man's individual needs and the needs of a society plagued by the consequences of changing values, alienation, hostility between generations, racial and international tensions, and the challenges of a new leisure.

Music educators at Tanglewood agreed that:

1. Music serves best when its integrity as an art is maintained.
2. Music of all periods, styles, forms, and cultures belong in the curriculum. The musical repertory should be expanded to involve music of our time in its rich variety, including currently popular

teenage music and avant-garde music, American folk music, and the music of other cultures.

3. Schools and colleges should provide adequate time for music in programs ranging from preschool through adult or continuing education.
4. Instruction in the arts should be a general and important part of education in the senior high school.
5. Developments in educational technology, educational television, programmed instruction, and computer-assisted instruction should be applied to music study and research.
6. Greater emphasis should be placed on helping the individual student to fulfill his needs, goals, and potentials.
7. The music education profession must contribute its skills, proficiencies, and insights toward assisting in the solution of urgent social problems as in the "inner city" or other areas with culturally deprived individuals.
8. Programs of teacher education must be expanded and improved to provide music teachers who are specially equipped to teach high school courses in the history and literature of music, courses in the humanities and related arts, and music teachers equipped to work with the very young, with adults, with the disadvantaged, and with the emotionally disturbed. (Choate 1968, 139)

The Goals and Objectives Project (GO Project)

The Goals and Objectives Project was begun in 1969 to implement the recommendations of the Tanglewood Symposium. The project, led by Paul Lehman, developed four major goals and thirty-five specific objectives. The goals were to: carry out comprehensive music programs in all schools; involve persons of all ages in learning music; support the quality preparation of teachers; and use the most effective techniques and resources in music instruction. The national executive board singled out eight of the objectives for immediate attention:

1. Lead in efforts to develop programs of music instruction challenging to all students, whatever their sociocultural condition in a pluralistic society.
2. Lead in the development of programs of study that correlate performing, creating, and listening to music and encompass a diversity of musical behaviors.

3. Assist teachers in the identification of musical behaviors relevant to the needs of their students.
4. Advance the teaching of music of all periods, styles, forms, and cultures.
5. Develop standards to ensure that all music instruction is provided by teachers well prepared in music.
6. Expand its [MENC] programs to secure greater involvement and commitment of student members.
7. Assume leadership in the application of significant new developments in curriculum, teaching-learning patterns, evaluation, and related topics, to every area and level of music teaching.
8. Lead in efforts to ensure that every school system allocates sufficient staff, time, and funding to support a comprehensive and excellent music program.

MENC Commissions

MENC has influenced American music education through its publications. The creation of *Source Book*s I and II involved thousands of members. *Music in General Education* is an example of a small group of experienced educators from across the country pooling their ideas. *The Study of Music in the Elementary School: A Conceptual Approach* represented a different configuration in which members from several school systems in a geographical area (southern California) shared the responsibilities of the assignment.

Two New Commissions

Two commissions were appointed to carry out the recommendations of the GO Project. The MENC Commission on Organizational Development was to prepare the way for changes in MENC's organization, structure, and function.

The National Commission on Instruction was created to monitor the way music was being taught in the schools. It published a critically important book, *The School Music Program: Description and Standards*. This book enabled communities to evaluate all aspects of their music programs. The commission revised the book in 1986. The publication had tangible results, as school systems throughout the country made efforts to reach at least the basic level recommended in the report. Paul Lehman said:

> *The School Music Program: Description and Standards* . . . has been used extensively by superintendents and principals, state departments of

education and state supervisors of music, music educators, and laymen. It has been referred to and quoted by various groups concerned with accreditation or certification, and it has been cited in innumerable curriculum guides. It has been the most popular publication in the history of MENC. (Lehman 1986, 7)

The Bicentennial Commission under the leadership of Don Robinson of Atlanta was appointed to suggest ways that music education might contribute to the nation's 200th birthday. The group prepared materials to assist music teachers in celebrating the occasion, including a large calendar of historical events. The J. C. Penney Corporation published a collection of American music, some of which it had commissioned for the occasion. It then gave the collection to schools in communities where it had stores.

The MENC Historical Center

President Paul Van Bodegraven wanted MENC to preserve its historical material and collect oral histories of older members. MENC and the University of Maryland came to an agreement, and official MENC papers are stored there along with a huge collection of documents, textbooks, and photographs of historical interest. Curator Bruce C. Wilson collected much oral history on tape. He became head music librarian at the University of Maryland in 1995, and Bonnie Jo Dopp was appointed Curator of Special Collections in Performing Arts in 1996. Vincent J. Novara became curator in 2006.

TOPICS FOR THOUGHT
AND DISCUSSION

1. Why did new education organizations form?
2. What motivated certain people to become professional leaders?
3. Discuss the direction the music education profession might have taken if MSNC had not been founded.
4. What are the most important contributions of MSNC/MENC?
5. What new direction did MENC take from the 1950s on?
6. What was the effect of the Tanglewood Symposium?
7. What have been the benefits to the music education profession of its research effort?

REFERENCES

Aiken. 1926. Letter to N. R. Crozier (family files).

American Association of School Administrators. 1959. *Official Report.* Washington, DC: AASA.

American Federation of Musicians. 1947. *For Understanding and Cooperation between School and Professional Musicians.* Code adopted by the American Federation of Musicians, MENC, and AASA. Chicago, September 22.

Annett, Thomas. 1939. "State Supervisors of Public School Music." *Music Educators Journal* 26.

———. 1955. "The Status of Rural School Music: A Survey." In *Music in American Education.* Chicago: Music Educators National Conference.

Arts in the Comprehensive High School. 1962. Washington, DC: National Association of Secondary School Principals.

Barnard, Henry, and C. W. Bardeen. 1909. *Proceedings of the National Teachers Association from Its Foundation in 1857 to the Sessions of 1879.* Syracuse: National Education Association.

Bartholomew, Marshall, and Robert Lawrence. 1920. *Music for Everybody: Organization and Leadership of Community Music Activities.* New York: Abingdon Press.

Basic Concepts in Music Education, Yearbook 57, pt. 2. 1909. Chicago: National Society for the Study of Education.

Birge, Edward Bailey. 1966. *History of Public School Music in the United States.* Washington, DC: Music Educators National Conference.

Britton, Allen P. 1984. "Founding *Journal of Research in Music Education:* A Personal View." *Journal of Research in Music Education* 32.

Buttelman, Clifford V. 1955. "Dedication." In *Music in American Education.* Washington, DC: Music Educators National Conference.

———, ed. 1962. *Will Earhart: A Steadfast Philosophy.* Washington, DC: Music Educators National Conference.

Channon, Chester N. 1959. "The Contributions of Philip Cady Haydn to Music Education in the United States." PhD dissertation, University of Michigan.

Choate, Robert A., ed. 1968. *Music in American Society: Documentary Report of the Tanglewood Symposium.* Washington, DC: Music Educator's National Conference.

Clark, Frances Elliott. 1933. "Music Appreciation and the New Day." *Music Educators Journal.*

Code of Ethics. 1947. *For Understanding and Cooperation between School and Professional Musicians.* Chicago: AF of M, MENC, AASA.

Colwell, Richard, ed. 1992. *Handbook of Research on Music Teaching and Learning.* New York: Schirmer Books.

———. 2002. *The New Handbook of Research on Music Teaching and Learning.* New York: Schirmer Books.

116   *Chapter 3*

Condon, Randall J. 1922. "A Supervisor as Seen by Superintendent." *Journal of Proceedings of the Fifteenth Annual Meeting of the Music Supervisors National Conference.* Ann Arbor, MI: Ann Arbor Press.

Cooper, Shelley. 2005. "Marguerite V. Hood and Music Education Radio Broadcasts in Rural Montana (1937–39)." *Journal of Research in Music Education.*

Earhart, Will. 1944. "A Tribute to a Colleague." *Music Educators Journal* 30 (May–June).

———. 1950. "A Philosophical Basis for Aesthetic Values in Education." *Music Educators Journal* 37.

Ernst, Karl D., and Charles L. Gary, eds. 1965. *Music in General Education.* Washington, DC: Music Educators National Conference.

Gary, Charles L. 1951. "History of Music Education in the Cincinnati Public Schools." PhD dissertation, University of Cincinnati.

Grant, Richard. 1940. "The New Constitution." *Yearbook of the Music Educators National Conference 30.* Chicago: Music Educators National Conference.

Journal of Proceedings and Addresses of the National Education Association, Boston, MA. 1903. Winona, MN: National Education Association.

Journal of Proceedings of the Eleventh Annual Meeting of the Music Supervisors National Conference. 1920. Madison: Music Supervisors National Conference.

Journal of Proceedings of the Music Educators National Conference. 1940. Chicago: Music Educators National Conference.

Journal of Proceedings of the Music Supervisors National Conference. 1929. Ithaca, NY: Music Supervisor's National Convention.

Kegerris, Richard. 1966. "Flint Central Launches the High School A Cappella Movement." *Journal of Research in Music Education* 14 (4).

Keokuk Daily Gate City, April 10, 11, 12, 1907.

Kindergarten and Its Relation to Elementary Education, Yearbook 6. 1907. National Society for the Study of Education.

Lehman, Paul R. 1986. *The School Music Program: Description and Standards.* 2nd ed. Reston, VA: Music Educators National Conference.

Lendrim, Frank T. 1962. "Music for Every Child: The Story of Karl Wilson Gehrkens." PhD dissertation, University of Michigan.

Maddy, Joseph E. 1929. "The Introduction and Development of Instrumental Music." Hartford: MSNC.

Mark, Michael L. 1980. "Music Educators National Conference and World War II Home Front Programs." *Bulletin of Historical Research in Music Education* 1.

Mark, Michael L., and Charles L. Gary. 2007. *A History of American Music Education.* 3rd ed. Lanham, MD: Rowman & Littlefield Education.

McConathy, Osbourne. 1919. "The Place of Public School Music in the Educational Program." *Proceedings of the Music Supervisors National Conference.* St. Louis: The Conference.

McConathy, Osbourne, W. Otto Miessner, Edward Bailey Birge, and Mabel E. Bray. 1933. *Music in Rural Education.* New York: Silver, Burdett.

McCoy's Keokuk City Directory. 2007.

Molnar, John W. 1954. "The Organization and Development of the Sectional Conference." *Journal of Research in Music Education* 1 (3).

———. 1955. "The Establishment of the Music Supervisors National Conference 1907–1910." *Journal of Research in Music Education* 3 (1).

Morgan, Hazel Nohavec. 1955. *Music in American Education.* Chicago: Music Educators National Conference.

Murphy, Judith, and George Sullivan. 1967. *Music in American Society.* Washington, DC: Music Educators National Conference.

Music Education, Yearbook 35. 1936. Chicago: National Society for the Study of Education.

Music Supervisors Journal. May 1915; September 1915; March 1916; November 1916; September 1918; September 1919; September 1921; October 1922; February 1923; May 1926; May 1930.

Platt, Melvin C., Jr. 1971. "Osbourne McConathy: American Music Educator." PhD dissertation, University of Michigan.

Roberts, John T. 1969. "Music Educators National Conference's Associated Organizations: NAJE." *Music Educators Journal.*

School Music. September 1904; October 1904; November 1904; May 1907; January 1908; May 1902.

Schwartz, Charles Frederick, Jr. 1966. "Edward Bailey Birge: His Life and Contributions to Music Education." PhD dissertation, Indiana University.

Stoddard, E. M. 1968. "Frances Elliott Clark: Her Life and Contributions to Music Education." EdD dissertation, Brigham Young University.

Warren, Fred Anthony. 1984. "A History of the Journal of Research in Music Education, 1953-65." *Journal of Research in Music Education* 33.

Wilson, Bruce, and Charles L. Gary. 1988. "Music in Our Schools: The First 150 Years." *Music Educators Journal* 74.

4

THE BROADENING
MUSIC CURRICULUM

THE HIGH SCHOOL

The high school came into being late in the nineteenth century, and four part choral singing was its primary music activity. Other music experiences—listening lessons, instrumental performing groups, music history, theory—began to appear in isolated places near the turn of the twentieth century. They were extra curricular at first and later evolved into separate curricular subjects.

In 1906, Leo Lewis of Tufts College made an informal report to the NEA Department of Music Education on the work planned by the Music Committee of the New England Education League (Birge 1928, 64). A. T. Manchester, president of the Music Teachers National Association, and professors at New England colleges were the committee members. Three NEA representatives, Benjamin Jepson, C. A. Fullerton, and Julia Etta Crane, were appointed to work with the League as it developed a high school course of study in music. At the Saint Louis meeting of NEA, Jepson distributed the framework for a four-year course of study. It included one hour of music four days each week, in addition to the usual weekly one hour of required choral music. Schools that adopted the plan would have music programs on a par with other disciplines (*Music Supervisors Journal* 1904, 702–7).

ACADEMIC CREDIT FOR MUSIC

When Superintendent of Schools F. B. Dyer welcomed the MSNC convention to Cincinnati in 1910, he asked for advice on two issues: the introduction of high school music appreciation, and students who wanted high school credit for studying music at either of the city's two conservatories or with members of the Cincinnati Symphony Orchestra. Will Earhart, Hollis Dann, Walter Aiken, Edward B. Birge, and Karl Gehrkens were appointed to develop a high school music course.[1] The next year, 1911, they recommended that credit be given for music study in high school. The practice of granting full credit for music courses requiring homework and laboratory, and one-half credit for rehearsals, originated with that report. There were isolated earlier cases, however, of credit for music study. Rock Island, Illinois, schools gave credit toward graduation as early as 1898 for instrumental music (Brown 1916–1917, 12). Other early examples of credit for orchestral participation were Richmond, Indiana (1912), Cincinnati (1914), and Parsons, Kansas (1920).

MUSIC APPRECIATION

Shortly before the turn of the twentieth century, Frances Elliott Clark spent ten minutes of each chorus rehearsal with her Ottumwa, Iowa, students telling them about composers and helping them recognize the historical stylistic features of their music. Will Earhart had his orchestra members in Richmond, Indiana, concentrate on sixteen composers. George Oscar Bowen offered an appreciation course for credit in Northampton, Massachusetts. Teachers who were good pianists were able to play for their students. When American engineer Edwin Votey patented a mechanical piano in 1897, another means of presenting music became available (Keith and Shepherd 1926, np).

Frances Elliott Clark described her introduction to the classroom potential of the phonograph. She heard the voice of Welsh singer Evan Williams coming from a phonograph in a music store. He was singing "All Through the Night," the same song she had been teaching her elementary students that week. She recognized how profoundly different her classroom would be if she had this new tool for teaching music. Clark became an authority on the use of the phonograph to teach music to children, and in 1910 she spoke to the Wisconsin Teachers Association on Victrolas in the Schools. Less than a year later she moved to Camden, New Jersey, to create the Education Department of the Victor Talking Machine Company. She supervised the recordings for the music classroom and she created recordings to correlate music with English and American literature. She also worked with retailers to set up displays to help music educators learn the benefits of the phonograph. Clark wrote:

---

1. This meant a major in music.

Music should be the concomitant of every day's experience in a child's life at home and in school—not only the music period, but permeating every phase of his activity and development. The need is great, and the material offered with the Victrola and Victor records is rich in volume, usefulness, and adaptability. If we have pointed out the road for millions of American children, and if we have led the way to a new field of the child's fairyland which shall grow with him to manhood's most beautiful playground of the soul, our highest hopes will have been fulfilled. (Clark 1920, 11)

Clark remained with Victor for the rest of her professional career, and she kept up with the times in the 1920s, when she promoted the radio as another avenue to music appreciation.

As the phonograph became a popular teaching tool in schools, Thaddeus Giddings took a dim view of the new technology: "It seems to me you supervisors ought to have a college education and you ought to have a voice. If you haven't a voice, you haven't any business being supervisors of music and we don't need a Victor machine—with all respect to Victor—but we don't need it if we are doing our duty the way we ought to do it." Obviously, Giddings was unable to hold back the tide of new technology that was finding its way into the schools.

THE RADIO

Alice Keith of the Cleveland schools and D. C. Boyle of the Ohio School of the Air were pioneers in the use of radio for teaching music. Keith wrote *Listening in on the Masters*, a music appreciation course to be used with radio and records (Keith and Shepherd 1926). She collaborated with Arthur Shepherd, Director of Young People's Concerts for the Cleveland Orchestra. MSNC President Edgar B. Gordon used the radio for a statewide music program in Wisconsin in 1917. He devised materials and techniques for effective music teaching via radio (Barresi 1987, 259). Walter Damrosch introduced millions of school children to classical music in 1928, when he broadcast *In the Hall of the Mountain King, The Sorcerer's Apprentice, Omphale's Spinning Wheel,* and *The Flying Dutchman.*

Marguerite Hood promoted three radio programs in the 1930s for rural students in Montana. She recommended Walter Damrosch's Friday morning NBC program, *Music Appreciation Hour.* Teachers received advance lists of music to be played, instructor manuals, and student notebooks. Hood also recommended the NBC program *Alice in Orchestralia,* broadcast on Friday afternoons, and the Thursday noon program, *Standard Symphony Hour* which offered a free teacher's manual from the Standard Oil Company of California. The *Symphony Hour* was coordinated with an evening concert broadcast on the same stations (Cooper 2005, 299). Elizabeth Beach gave a series of Christmas carol festivals on the CBS Radio Network beginning in 1931. She utilized thousands of students from the Syracuse elementary, high schools, and normal school. There were forty boys in the chorus in 1931 and seven hundred by the end of the decade (Beach family records).

In 1912, Will Earhart became director of music for the Pittsburgh, Pennsylvania, schools. He and Birge prepared four books in a series entitled *Master Musicians* (the Richmond course), which C. C. Birchard published in 1909. Both men had been intensely interested in appreciation as early as the turn of the century. In addition to the many helpful publications that Frances Clark issued from the Victor Company, other books appeared on the market to help students, teachers, and the general public become better listeners. Some of the best were prepared by Lillian Baldwin in connection with her radio broadcasts and the Children's Concerts of the Cleveland Orchestra, which began in 1929. In time, student textbooks began to include appreciation material.

MUSIC APPRECIATION AND PROGRESSIVE EDUCATION

Many of the early music appreciation books were structured according to principles of progressive education, especially in terms of the three stages of child development. The stages were the Sensory Period (grades 1–3), the Associative Period (grades 4–6), and the Adolescent Period (grades 7–12). Books like Agnes Moore Fryberger's *Listening Lessons in Music: Graded for Schools* were divided into sections that corresponded to the three periods (Fryberger 1916, 181). Frances Elliot Clark's book *Music Appreciation for Little Children* was designed to meet the needs of the child's mind during the sensory period of development.

INSTRUMENTAL MUSIC

Instrumental music in the public schools began in the middle of the nineteenth century, when the American public was introduced to touring orchestras and bands. The orchestras and bands were loved by the American public, and were the models for school orchestras and bands.

One of the most familiar figures in American instrumental music was Theodore Thomas (1825–1905), a violinist who was born in Germany and emigrated to America with his parents when he was ten years old. Thomas recognized that the only way to build an American orchestra of European standards was to hire the best musicians and provide them with steady activity. The Theodore Thomas Orchestra played in almost every community of any size. For countless Americans, their first exposure to a good orchestra playing the finest orchestral literature was the Theodore Thomas Orchestra. He directed the Cincinnati May Festival from 1873 to 1905 and was the first president of the College of Music of Cincinnati. Thomas became conductor of the New York Philharmonic Society, and then founded the Chicago Symphony Orchestra. He conducted the Chicago Symphony until 1905, the year of his death.

Concert Bands

Early American orchestras were modeled after European orchestras, but the professional bands were not. The concert bands met a different social need than the orchestras. Bands like Gilmore's and Sousa's entertained their audiences with superb showmanship. They met the popular needs of the people while the orchestras maintained the traditions of the Old World.

The Development of School Bands and Orchestras (1900–1935)

School bands and orchestras are examples of the interaction between school and industry. The music, entertainment, and transportation industries all contributed to a major development in school music. The several threads of this story are woven together by the interests of the musical instrument manufacturers, whose businesses prospered or suffered according to the number of school, professional, military, and community bands that needed to purchase instruments.

School orchestras preceded bands. As early as 1896 there was a grammar school orchestra at Nathan Hale School in New London, Connecticut, and at other Connecticut schools. Jesse Clark formed an orchestra in Wichita, Kansas, in 1896 (Birge 1937, 162). Will Earhart created a high school orchestra two years later in Richmond, Indiana, that was known for its complete instrumentation and its high musical standards (Birge 1937, 162).

Joseph Maddy is believed to have been the first Supervisor of Instrumental Music in the country in 1918 in Rochester, New York. Maddy, an excellent teacher and powerful advocate for his program, persuaded George

Eastman to donate $10,000 worth of instruments to the Rochester schools. The money allowed Maddy to create a model program.[2] Cincinnati, Ohio, and Oakland, California, established instrumental music programs early in the 1920s. Oakland, California, and Rochester, New York, had begun to offer wind instrument instruction in 1917. Louis Aiken organized the first high school band in Cincinnati in 1919 at Hughes High School.

Instrumental music and progressive education complemented each other. Playing in a band or orchestra was believed to lead to character development, healthy leisure activities, and socialization. It also promoted democratic values and citizenship through participation in civic events and playing patriotic music. These benefits resonated with progressive goals. Bands and orchestras kept boys (but usually not girls) occupied with a productive activity and in many cases provided the education and experience necessary for them to become professional musicians.

The performance of Joseph Maddy's Richmond High School Orchestra at the 1922 MSNC meeting led to the creation of the Committee on Instrumental Affairs. Jay W. Fay of Rochester was named chairman, and Russell Morgan, acting director of music in Cleveland, Victor Rebmann, B. F. Stuber, and Eugene Hahnel were members. MSNC had given little attention to school bands until then. In 1922, it began to focus on instrumental music in schools.

It was clear that a centralized effort was needed to create a nationwide movement for instrumental music in schools. That effort was provided by the musical instrument manufacturers at a critical time in the growth of their industry.

The Professional Concert Bands and the Amusement Parks

One of the most popular venues for the professional bands was the amusement parks, of which there were hundreds throughout the United States. The bands played concert and dance music at the parks. The concert band was well-suited for the dances of the time—the schottische, polka, waltz, and two-step.[3] Unfortunately for the bands, the public's taste in dancing changed during the first two decades of the twentieth century; less

---

2. This was Eastman's first philanthropic venture. He was so enthusiastic about school music that it became one of his deepest interests after the photographic industry that he founded. Also in 1918, Eastman talked about founding a school of music in Rochester. The Eastman School of Music opened in 1921, thanks to Eastman's philanthropy.

3. John Philip Sousa's "Washington Post March" was commonly used as a two-step dance. Dancers in other countries referred to the two-step as a Washington Post.

polite dances like the Charleston, jitterbug, fox trot, and black bottom became popular. Small dance bands or jazz bands were suited for these dances, not the large concert bands.

Change was in the air—radical and profound change that made the United States a very different country from what it had been only a decade before. The amusement parks were called "trolley parks," or "end of the line trolley parks," because they were usually located outside of cities at the end of a trolley line. Usually, the owners of the parks also owned the trolley lines. The trolley parks were weekend destinations for countless millions throughout the United States who were unable to go elsewhere because they had no other means of transportation. People relaxed at the parks, rode the roller coaster, the Ferris wheel and merry-go-round, and enjoyed the casino, paddle boats, food, concerts, and dancing to the music of concert bands. The trolley parks were one of the most successful forms of American entertainment at that time.

Times changed as the automobile became available to the public. Henry Ford envisioned a population whose new mobility would transform society. He began selling the Model T Ford, called the "flivver" or "tin lizzie" in 1908 ("You can have it any color, so long as it's black") for as little as $850. Now an automobile owner could go anywhere he desired. As the trolley park business declined, so did the professional concert bands, and so did band instrument sales.

The army created many new bands during World War I, and when the war ended in 1918, the military bandleaders transferred their musical skills to civilian life. Many became school music teachers. Others played in vaudeville theaters, but vaudeville was in its declining years, and by then small dance bands were playing the fox trot, rhumba, *paso doble*, shag, big apple, Charleston, black bottom, and Lindy hop. There was no room for concert bands in the new era of social dancing. Radio and recordings also competed with the concert bands. The new media attracted millions of listeners and were a major factor in the decline of professional concert bands. The concert bands could no longer compete for the attention of music lovers.

With ever-decreasing sales to the military and professional bands, the manufacturers turned their attention to school bands. The companies aligned themselves with school music by helping to create band competitions. It was natural for competitions to develop as school bands proliferated. State and county fairs had offered early venues for band competitions. William V. Arvold, a history teacher in Reedsburg, Wisconsin, organized a high school band in 1919 and planned a tournament involving three other bands the following year (Fonder 1989, 112–13). The involvement of the Holton Band

Instrument Company of Elkhorn, Indiana, the next year solidly established the band contest. Holton and several other companies donated instruments as prizes for the 1921 school band contest at Elkhorn.

The 1923 music trades convention in Chicago included a tournament (Holz 1962, 3–12). Thirty bands participated, and each was allowed to select its own pieces. The only judge was William H. Santelmann, director of the U.S. Marine Corps Band. John W. Wainwright's Fostoria, Ohio, high school band won the first place ribbon and a thousand dollars.

The Instrumental Affairs Committee

C. M. Tremaine, head of the National Bureau for the Advancement of Music, suggested that educators, rather than manufacturers, should handle contests to avoid the appearance of exploiting students, and after that the MSNC Instrumental Affairs Committee governed future contests. The committee prepared a repertoire list of literature that the average band would play in 1924 and required that contest selections be taken from the committee's list. The contests led to the standardization of band instrumentation, the practice of publishing full band scores instead of piano reductions, increased emphasis on instrumental music in teacher training programs, and the dramatic growth of school bands.

Orchestra and choir contests soon joined the movement. The first national orchestra contest was held in Iowa City in 1929, and the National School Band Association expanded to become the National School Band and Orchestra Association. It changed again to become the National School Band, Orchestra and Vocal Association. In 1932, the organization divided into two groups, and in 1936, the National School Vocal Association was formed. By then there were three organizations—band, orchestra, and vocal—and all became separate auxiliaries of the Music Educators National Conference.

School administrators became concerned about events that had one winner and many losers. They agreed that competitive events resulted in high levels of musical performance, but they wanted a change. In 1933, ratings replaced rankings. The national contests were suspended during World War II and were never resumed. In 1952, the regional system was eliminated and the state level became the highest level for interscholastic MENC events.

Bands and Their Communities

An officer of the National Bureau for the Advancement of Music commented during the contest movement that "a good school band can add more than perhaps anything else to the prestige of its school and town."

The early career of William D. Revelli, a towering figure in college bands, dramatically illustrates the point. His first full-time teaching job was Supervisor of Music for the elementary and high schools of the small town of Hobart, Indiana, from 1925 to 1935. He was hired to teach singing at all levels from kindergarten through high school, and to direct the high school choir. The Hobart schools had no instrumental program.

Two weeks after he started at Hobart, Revelli received permission to begin an instrumental music program. It had no budget, no time in the schedule, and no rehearsal room, but the new band rehearsed three days a week, from 7:00 to 8:00 AM, in a chemistry classroom. The orchestra rehearsed in the same room from 4:00 to 5:15 PM two days a week. From this inauspicious beginning in October 1925 grew a band that gave its first concert in January 1926. By 1930, the band was performing difficult music like Rossini's *Barber of Seville Overture,* Flotow's *Stradella Overture,* Alford's *Colonel Bogey March,* and Lalo's *Spanish Symphony* (Mark 1980, 7).

Indiana was, and still is, known as a basketball state. Hobart was no exception, but as its high school band developed into a mature organization, the town realized that its basketball team was paralleled by its band. Revelli led the band to first place in the national contests for five consecutive years. The Hobart High School Band was a source of tremendous community pride. George Cavanaugh discussed Revelli's influence:

> After 1930, each student was at least as strongly motivated by fear that the band might lose. The band had established a reputation—Hobart was expected to win, and winning became a tradition which had to be upheld at each subsequent contest. . . . After 1930, any other rating would have been considered a failure—a personal failure for every band member, a failure to maintain the tradition of the Hobart band, and a failure to meet the expectations of the community which supported the band. (Cavanaugh 1971, 7)

The success of the Hobart band occurred during the Great Depression. The schools closed a month early when the city ran out of funds. Revelli took advantage of his students' extra time by rehearsing the band six hours a day for the national contest. Community support for the band was so high that it was able to raise funds for the band to buy uniforms and to travel during the Great Depression. Even the Hobart Athletic Club occasionally donated half of the basketball gate receipts to the band. Cavanaugh said:

> When the people in Hobart discovered the kind of band director they had, there was almost nothing they wouldn't do for him. Did you know

that some of those people actually spent less money on their own food so they could help the band? He was worthy of that kind of support, because he gave his students something to remember for the rest of their lives. He made the whole town proud of itself. (Cavanaugh 1971, 7)

The intensity of Hobart's pride in its high school band was echoed in communities throughout the country. The high school band movement solidified during these years, and bands have constituted an integral part of school and community life to this day.

School Orchestras

A grammar school orchestra existed at Nathan Hale School in New London, Connecticut, as early as 1896, and several New Britain and Hartford schools had elementary orchestras (Monnier 1904, 25). The orchestra that Will Earhart built at the high school in Richmond, Indiana, beginning in 1898, was important because it was an early school orchestra with symphonic instrumentation and high musical standards. Joseph Maddy maintained those standards when he replaced Earhart at Richmond. That orchestra led to the creation of both the National High School Orchestra and the National Music Camp at Interlochen, Michigan. Other orchestras were well-developed before the Richmond orchestra played at the 1922 MSNC program in Nashville, but it was that appearance that inspired many teachers to establish new high school orchestras.

In 1926, Maddy formed the first National High School Orchestra to perform for the Detroit meeting of MSNC. The orchestra consisted of 236 high school musicians from thirty states. Maddy organized the Second National High School Orchestra in 1927 to perform for the Department of Superintendence of the National Education Association in Dallas. The superintendents were so impressed that they adopted a resolution recommending that music and art everywhere receive equal consideration with other subjects.

The following year, Maddy organized the National High School Orchestra for the third time to play for the Chicago MSNC meeting. Several of the musicians played with the orchestra for the third time. They were so enthusiastic that Maddy, with his close associate, Thaddeus P. Giddings, decided to search for a summer home for the orchestra. With the assistance of many musicians, educators, philanthropists, and education foundations, Maddy and Giddings founded the National High School Orchestra and

Band Camp at Interlochen, Michigan. It has grown from its humble beginnings to a prestigious year-round arts academy that attracts outstanding students and faculty from many countries.

Albert G. Mitchell

The curate of the parish church in Maidstone, England, whose identity is unknown, formed the first violin class with children around 1905 (Deverich 1987, 39–55). Albert Mitchell, an Englishman who taught music in the Boston schools, traveled to England in 1910 to observe class violin instruction in Maidstone. He was impressed with the program and when he returned to Boston, he organized five classes of violin students with sixteen to twenty students in each class. The free lessons were so successful that after two years he became a full-time teacher of instrumental music. He published the *Violin Class Method* in 1924, and later wrote class methods for cello, cornet, trombone, and clarinet.

Charles Farnsworth

Charles Farnsworth, of Columbia University, studied education practices in Germany, Switzerland, France, and England. He agreed with "the advantages of everyone knowing 20 or 30 songs or chorals," a practice he found in Germany. Peter Dykema suggested the practice to the supervisors at the 1913 Rochester convention (*Musical Herald* 1913, 5, 9). Farnsworth's appreciation of the educational value of Emile Jaques-Dalcroze's use of improvisation created another path for American music education. His description of the Maidstone project in England was the key to the explosion of instrumental music in American public schools (Birge 1937, 189).

Heterogeneous Class Teaching

Twentieth century music teachers who wanted to form bands and orchestras did not have enough time to offer class instruction on separate instruments. Some developed materials and techniques to teach several instruments in one class. The best-known method book for this purpose was *The Universal Teacher* by Joseph Maddy and Thaddeus Giddings, published in 1923. All of the instruments were given equal importance and all had melodies to play. *The Universal Teacher* was widely adopted.

Elementary School Orchestras

High schools usually had orchestras before elementary schools. In 1913 the lower schools in Cincinnati had eight orchestras, three years after the high school orchestra was officially recognized as a curricular subject. In the early 1920s, all-city orchestras drawn from eleven elementary schools played for conventions of the Federation of Mothers Clubs and the Western Arts Association. The contest movement and well-planned advertising campaigns by the instrument manufacturers supported school orchestras and bands as their numbers increased. "Gee, Dad! It's a Wurlitzer" became part of the language of musical instruments and eventually a gag line for comedians and cartoonists.

The Marching Band

The marching band originated in the military and began to appear in schools around the turn of the twentieth century. In 1905, Austin A. Harding became director of the University of Illinois Band, where he founded the Department of Bands.[4] At that time, high school and college marching bands were ragged, untrained aggregations of instrumentalists. Harding said, "When we first began to form letters and words . . . we had never seen or heard of a college band which formed words while marching and playing." Bands throughout the country imitated Harding's Illinois band, which was the most influential force in the development of high school marching bands. He was also a key figure in the improvement of concert bands.

The marching band eventually became an important public relations tool for schools. In 1932, Mark Hindsley wrote:

> The value of the marching band to music education in general lies in its advertising power. It provides a strong incentive to all youth to study music so as to participate in band activities. Parents are quick to realize the worth of such an organization in a disciplinary way and as an outlet for some of the child's leisure time and surplus energy.

Music Memory Contests

In 1923, Julia D. Owen, chair of the Public School Music Committee of the Texas Music Clubs, conducted a statewide survey about the musical memory contest (*Music Supervisors Journal* February 1923, 40). The contests offered all students the opportunity to participate, and the survey revealed

---

4. Harding wanted more freedom than he would have had under the music department.

that students in thirty-four schools had been drilled. The contests swept the country, possibly because it reminded parents of the spelling bees during their own school days. Parents drilled their children to help them prepare, and no other aspect of music education involved the family like the music memory contests. Newspapers published lists of works to be used in the contests. Theater orchestras and organists played the contest music between film showings to give their young patrons one more chance to familiarize themselves with the melodies. Fifty radio stations played the music on the National Contest List (Fisher 1926, 8–16). Mr. And Mrs. Max Oberndorfer, both pianists, broadcast the music for the Chicago contest. The Victor Talking Machine Company sent a free booklet to anyone conducting a contest. The booklet listed 250 standard selections that might be used.

The memory contests coincided with the community music movement and reinforced the positive feelings of the public toward school music and MSNC's goal to make America musical. By the late 1920s, most homes had a radio, the movies were no longer silent, and the memory contests became a thing of the past.

Musical Discrimination Contests

In the early 1930s, MSNC sponsored a contest of musical discrimination. Walter Damrosch played ten musical selections over the National Broadcasting Company network, and NBC offered scholarships to three winners. For each composition, students were asked to identify the style of the music and to suggest a possible composer; they also answered questions about form and the solo instruments, and they would give an appropriate name to a piece of program music. Fifty-four of the seventy-five best papers came from members of the National High School Orchestra and the National High School Chorus.

TEACHER EDUCATION

At the 1902 meeting of the NEA Department of Music Education in Minneapolis, Thomas Tapper of Boston, A. J. Gantwoort of Cincinnati, and O. T. Corson of Columbus served on a committee to formulate a plan of study for music teachers (*Journal* 1902, 626). They proposed standards that have existed in teacher training programs since:

1. literary qualification at least equal to those of high school graduates;

2. musical qualification to include proficiency on an instrument or as a singer, knowledge of theory, music history, and conducting;
3. familiarity with school music textbooks and courses of study.

Few colleges offered "public school music" courses at that time. *Etude* had advertisements in 1906 for public school music training programs at the Crane Normal Institute, Northwestern University, and the Detroit Conservatory. The American Conservatory in Chicago offered some lectures on the subject, and courses were available at teachers colleges. A. J. Gantwoort introduced a course for teachers at the College of Music of Cincinnati in 1894. The college and the schools had been connected through the May Festival since Theodore Thomas founded it. It was not until 1905 that the Cincinnati Conservatory offered a summer course in school music. It adopted a similar course as part of its winter curriculum in 1909.

There was concern in many states about the quality of teacher education, and a competition developed between the normal schools that were evolving into teachers colleges and the traditional colleges and universities. The first issue of *Music Supervisors Journal*, published in 1914, reported that several midwestern states were formulating regulations governing both school and private music teachers. Frank Beach of Kansas State Teachers College at Emporia reported in 1916 that many states required two years of college for school music supervisors and that "it may not be long before the states will require four years for music, as for other studies."

Curriculum

The first action of the newly established MSNC Educational Council in 1918 was to create a committee to develop a course for the training of supervisors of music. The recommended curriculum consisted of general education, professional education, and music. One quarter of the program of study was assigned to each of the first two, and the other half to applied and theoretical music. MSNC left the specifics of academic work and the proportion of theoretical and applied music to the individual institutions.

Teacher Preparation Materials

New materials were published in the second decade of the twentieth century. Hamlin E. Cogswell wrote *How to Teach Music in Public Schools: A Complete Outline; Graded, Un-Graded, High and Normal Schools* (1910). The sixty-page manual covered the goals and methods for grades 1 through 8, normal schools, music theory, and instrumental music. *The Teacher's Manual Music: Newly Revised and Enlarged Edition* (probably written by H. W. Fairbank in 1924) was only forty pages and covered music teaching from the first through the eighth grades. Some of the issues of that time still face music teachers. One was the monotone singer. Cogswell wrote in 1910, "Monotones *must not* be permitted to sing with the class. *Encourage—never tell a child he is a monotone,* this is a serious mistake. Never cease trying to help the non-singing pupil. Often the change comes suddenly."

A Pioneering Instrumental Music Teachers Preparation Program

William D. Revelli recognized that little attention was given to the education of school instrumental music teachers. He addressed the problem shortly after he joined the faculty of the University of Michigan in 1935 as chair of the Wind Instrument Department. At that time, little emphasis had been placed on wind instrument instruction, and universities did not have degree programs in wind instruments. As the demand increased for highly trained band directors, Revelli created a degree program in wind instruments for band directors who preferred not to enroll in the public school music program. Students majored in their primary instrument and were required to perform on all of the woodwind or brass instruments. The 1944–1945 *School of Music Announcement* stated, "The curriculum is designed to prepare students for a professional career as members or conductors of orchestras and bands, the specialized teaching of woodwind or brass wind instruments at the college level, and teaching positions in the larger secondary schools." The program led to the Bachelor of Music degree, and eventually masters and doctoral degree programs were offered by the department (Mark 1980, 16–17). It has been emulated by universities throughout the country.

TOPICS FOR THOUGHT AND DISCUSSION

1. Discuss the impact of technology—radio, recordings, player piano— on music education.
2. What were some of the problems of rural music education?
3. What was the stimulus for the creation of bands and orchestras?
4. Discuss how instrumental music might have developed if group teaching, rather than private teaching, had not developed.
5. What were some of the positives of the contest movement? Negatives?

REFERENCES

Barresi, Anthony L. 1987. "Edgar B. Gordon: A Pioneer in Media Music Education." *Journal of Research in Music Education* 35 (spring).

Beach, Elizabeth. Family records, in the Music Educators National Conference Historical Center, University of Maryland, College Park.

Birge, Edward Bailey. 1928. *History of Public School Music in the United States.* Washington, DC: Music Supervisors National Conference.

———. 1937. *A History of Public School Music in the United States.* Chicago: Music Educators National Conference.

Brown, Gladys A. 1916, 1917. "Report of Survey on Instrumental Music in Our Schools." *Music Supervisors Journal* 3 (November, January).

Bryant, Carolyn. 1975. *And the Band Played On: 1776–1976.* Washington, DC: The Smithsonian Institution Press.

Burdette, Noreen Diamond. 1985. "The High School Music Contest Movement in the United States." MusD dissertation, Boston University.

Burford, Cary Clive. 1952. "Band Formations and Pageantry at Football Games." *We're Loyal to You, Illinois.* Danville: Interstate Printers.

Cavanaugh, George. 1971. "William D. Revelli: The Hobart Years." PhD diss., University of Virginia.

Clark, Frances Elliott. 1920. *Music Appreciation for Little Children.* Camden, NJ: Victor Talking Machine Company.

———. 1926. *Music Appreciation with the Victrola for Children.* Camden, NJ: Victor Talking Machine Company.

Cooper, Shelley. 2005."Marguerite V. Hood and Music Education Radio Broadcasts in Rural Montana (1937–39)." *Journal of Research in Music Education* 53 (4): 295–307.

Cuban, Larry. 1984. *How Teachers Taught: Constancy and Change in American Classrooms, 1890–1980.* New York: Longman.

Damon, Inez Field. 1920. "Public School Piano Classes as I Have Known Them." *Journal of Proceedings of the Thirteenth Annual Meeting of the Music Supervisors National Conference.* Oberlin: Music Supervisors National Conference.

Deverich, Robin K. 1987. "The Maidstone Movement—Influential British Precursor of American Public School Instrumental Classes." *Journal of Research in Music Education* 35.

Dvorak, Raymond Francis. 1937. *The Band on Parade.* New York: Carl Fischer.

Dwight's Journal of Music. July 27, 1872; July 3, 1869; July 27, 1872.

Earhart, Will. 1921. *Music Supervisors Journal* 8.

Eliot, Charles W. 1910. *Introduction to Essays on Education and Kindred Subjects by Herbert Spencer.* New York: E. P. Dutton & Co.

Fennell, Frederick. 1954. *Time and the Winds: A Short History of the Use of Wind Instruments in the Orchestra, Band, and the Wind Ensemble.* Kenosha, WI: G. Leblanc Publications.

Fisher, William Arms. 1926. "The Radio and Music." *Music Supervisors Journal* 11 (February).

Fonder, Mark. 1989. "The Wisconsin School Music Association and Its Contests: The Early Years." *Journal of Research in Music Education* 37.

Fryberger, Agnes Moore. 1916. *Listening Lessons in Music: Graded for Schools.* Boston: Silver, Burdett and Company.

Goldman, Richard Franko. 1961. "Band Music in America." In *One Hundred Years of Music in America*, ed. Paul Henry Lang. New York: G. Schirmer, Inc.

Harding, Austin A. 1915. "The Band as a Community Asset." *Proceedings of the 38th Annual Meeting of the Music Teachers National Association.* Hartford: Music Teachers National Association.

Hindsley, Mark H. 1932. *Band—At-ten-tion! A Manual for the Marching Band.* Chicago: Gamble Hinged Music Co.

———. 1940. *School Band and Orchestra Administration.* Lynbrook, NY: Boosey & Hawkes.

Holz, Emil A. Spring 1962. "The School Band Contest of America." *Journal of Research in Music Education* 10.

Hood, Marguerite. 1936. "Can Festivals Take the Place of Contests?" *Music Educators Journal* 23.

Johnson, Paul. 1997. *A History of the American People.* New York: Harper Perennial.

Journals of 41st, 42nd, 43rd, and 44th Annual Meetings of the National Education Association, 1902, 1903, 1904, 1905.

Journal of Proceedings and Addresses of the Forty-Seventh Annual Meeting of the National Education Association. 1909. Denver: National Education Association.

Keene, James A. 1987. *Music and Education in Vermont.* Glenbridge, IL: Glenbridge Publishing Ltd.

Keith, Alice, and Arthur Shepherd. 1926. *Listening in on the Masters.* Boston: C.C. Birchard & Co.

Krone, Max. 1939. "Do Festival-Clinics Solve the Problem?" *Music Educators Journal* 26.

Lahee, Henry C. 1925. *The Orchestra.* Boston: The Boston Musical and Educational Bureau.

Lendrim, Frank T. 1962. "Music for Every Child: The Story of Karl Wilson Gehrken." EdD dissertation, The University of Michigan.

Mark, Michael L. Fall 1980. "William D. Revelli: Portrait of a Distinguished Career." *Journal of Band Research* 16.

———. 2002. *Music Education: Source Readings from Ancient Greece to Today.* 2nd ed. New York: Routledge.

Metz, Donald E. 1968. "A Critical Analysis of Selected Aspects of the Thought of James L. Mursell." PhD dissertation, Case Western University.

Mitchell, William G. 1920. *Journal of Proceedings of the Thirteenth Annual Meeting of the Music Supervisors National Conference.* Madison: Music Supervisors National Conference.

Molnar, John W. Spring 1955. "The History of the Music Educators National Conference." *Journal of Research in Music Education* 3.

Monnier, W. D. 1904. "Grammar School Orchestras." *School Music* 5.

Murphy, Judith, and George Sullivan. 1968. *Music in American Society*. Washington: Music Educators National Conference.

Mursell, James L. 1938. *The Psychology of School Music Teaching*. New York: Silver Burdett Company.

Music Supervisors Journal. 1904; November 1916; October 1922; February 1923.

Musical Herald. 1913. No additional information available.

Richman, Luther Anton. 1931. "The Cost to the Student of a Four-Year Course in Public School Music on the Collegiate Level." M.A. thesis in Education, University of Cincinnati.

School Index (Cincinnati). April 28, 1922. 8 (32).

Schwartz, H. W. 1957. *Bands of America*. Garden City, NJ: Doubleday & Company.

Seashore, Carl E. September 1919. "Measurement of Musical Talent." *Music Supervisors Journal*.

Spruill, Julia Cherry. 1972. *Women's Life & Work in the Southern Colonies*. New York: W. W. Norton & Co.

Stebbins, Lucy B., and Richard Stebbins. 1945. *Frank Damrosch: Let the People Sing*. Durham: Duke University Press.

Tapper, Thomas. 1914. *The Education of the Music Teacher*. Philadelphia: Theodore Presser Co.

Thorndike, Edward L. 1918. "The Nature, Purposes and General Methods of Measurement of Educational Products." *Seventeenth Yearbook*, Part II, National Society for the Study of Education. Bloomington, IL: Public School Publishing Co.

Warren, Frederick Anthony. 1966. "History of the Music Education Research Council and the *Journal of Research in Music Education*." EdD dissertation, The University of Michigan.

Wassell, Albert W. April–May 1954. "Albert Gore Mitchell: A Pioneer Class Instrumental Music Instructor in America." *Music Educators Journal* 40.

5

MUSIC EDUCATION EXPANDS

MID-TWENTIETH CENTURY

The United States emerged from World War II as the world's strongest military, economic, and industrial force. It helped other nations rebuild themselves after the war, while at the same time continuing its own momentum. This dual role generated a strong economy as the nation began to transform itself from an industrial society into an early technological society. The new age brought prosperity, but tension and anxiety came with it. When the Cold War began not long after the end of World War II, the Western world was divided between capitalism and communism. The Cold War created new demands on the United States.

Rapid, continuous change was a new phenomenon in American society. Never before had society changed so radically and with such speed. New information technology helped fuel a dramatic increase in information and knowledge, which in turn led to new innovations. The fast pace of change required a citizenry capable of leading the nation in the age of technology, but the schools were unprepared to meet that demand. Throughout the 1950s, industrial, military, and political leaders became increasingly alarmed by the weak education system.

In October 1957, the Soviet Union launched the first artificial orbiting satellite, Sputnik I. A sense of urgency overtook the United States as Americans feared that Soviet technological dominance would lead to another war. As the public became aware of the relationship between education and national security, school improvement became a national priority. A movement developed to reform the American education system. Admiral Hyman Rickover was one of the most vocal leaders of the movement. Rickover, having directed the development of the United States

Navy atomic submarine program, was familiar with the education needs of the technological age. He was highly respected and admired as a military leader who depended on an educated population to support his program. He made it clear that he thought Americans had become soft and undisciplined. Rickover was aware that Americans had a much higher standard of living than Soviet citizens and that the lack of intellectual freedom in the Soviet Union brought with it second rate art, literature, and theater. But he thought it more important to produce scientists and engineers to lead the scientific programs needed to maintain world leadership.

Rickover was a strident reformer with an elitist view of American education. He said that American schools were weak in comparison with European schools, which provided the necessary intellectual, cultural, and physical requirements. European students who could not meet the highest standards received vocational training. American schools attempted to educate all children equally, which Rickover considered a waste of precious resources. He wanted high ability given preference. He emphatically recommended that science and math offerings be strengthened and that frills be eliminated from the curriculum.

Dr. James Bryant Conant, former president of Harvard University, was another reformer who stressed stronger academic preparation. Unlike Rickover, Conant recommended in his book, *The American High School*, that students study the arts as well as mathematics and science (Conant 1959, 48). Rickover, Conant, and other reformers helped elevate public awareness of the problems that faced American education. They directed public attention to the weakness of academic programs in mathematics, science, foreign languages, and reading, which much of the public considered to be the basic subjects. Music and other subjects were perceived as frills by many people. As the federal government became more involved in education, the general public became more aware of the critical role its schools played in maintaining and improving the quality of American life and its world leadership role.

A key event, the Woods Hole Conference, took place in 1959 at Woods Hole, Massachusetts. Its purpose was to discuss the problems of science education and recommend solutions. Educators, historians, physicists, biologists, psychologists, and mathematicians attended. This conference was the beginning of a new trend—the unified efforts of distinguished people from related fields addressing themselves to the general improvement of education.

For the first time, the federal government became deeply involved in education. The late 1950s and early 1960s saw vast amounts of resources dedicated to the improvement of curricular areas directly related to the needs of American society. The arts were included in the new wave of funding but did not receive significant amounts of support.

Curricular Concerns

Education leaders considered the unbalanced curriculum dangerous, and the arts a necessary part of American education. The American Association of School Administrators issued the following statement in 1959:

> We believe in a well-balanced school curriculum in which music, drama, painting, poetry, sculpture, architecture and the like are included side by side with other important subjects such as mathematics, history, and science. It is important that pupils, as a part of general education, learn to appreciate, to understand, to create, and to criticize with discrimination those products of the mind, the voice, the hand, and the body which give dignity to the person and exalt the spirit of man. American Association of School Administrators, *Official Report for the Year* 1959, including a record of the Annual Meeting and Work Conference on Education and the Creative Arts. (American Association of School Administrators 1959, 248–49)

The National Education Association Project on Instruction also supported the arts in the curriculum. The project report stated:

> Priorities for the schools are the teaching of skills in reading, composition, listening, speaking (native and foreign languages), and computation . . . ways of creative and disciplined thinking . . . competence in self instruction and independent thinking . . . fundamental understanding of the humanities and the arts, the social sciences and the natural sciences, and in literature, music, and the visual arts. (Sand 1963, 101)

Scientists disagreed with the unbalanced curriculum. The Panel on Educational Research and Development, an advisory body of nongovernmental experts, recommended action to the National Science Foundation, the U.S. Office of Education, and the President's Office of Science and Technology:

> Certain members of the Panel were convinced that there was a degree of correlation between excellence in scientific achievement and the breadth of an individual's human experience. The best scientists, it was thought, were not necessarily those who had devoted themselves single-

mindedly to their own field; somehow, familiarity with the arts and humanities sharpened a good scientist's vision. (Lowens 1971, E4)

The 1960s brought significant changes to education. Scholastic Achievement Tests (SAT) scores improved. At the same time, music retained its place in the curriculum, in part because scientists, school administrators, and other influential people spoke for it. The baby boom that followed World War II brought heavy enrollments to schools, but there was a shortage of teachers for the new schools. Young people became involved in education policy through the 1960s youth movement, which led to an expanded curriculum. Teachers and administrators attempted to satisfy students by making schools more humanistic. They lowered academic requirements and designed courses that would allow students to "get in touch with their feelings" and "discover themselves." Many of the new courses were in soft areas like decision-making, attitudinal development, and survey courses in subjects of personal interest to students. Enrollments declined in traditional curricular areas like math, science, English, foreign languages, classical studies, and the arts.

A national accountability movement helped clarify goals and objectives and provided tools to measure the effectiveness of the schools. A highly publicized report, *A Nation at Risk: The Imperative for Education Reform* was reminiscent of the fears raised years earlier by Sputnik. The report was released in 1983 by the National Commission on Excellence in Education. Other reports, similar to *A Nation at Risk*, were issued by the Twentieth Century Fund Task Force on Federal Elementary and Secondary Education Policy; the National Task Force on Education for Economic Growth; the National Science Board Commission on Precollege Education in Mathematics, Science and Technology; the College Board; and the Carnegie Foundation for the Advancement of Teaching.

The reports agreed on the importance of the mastery of language and a core curriculum. They disagreed about the nature and meaning of the core curriculum. Some of the reports supported arts education, but the most prominent one, *A Nation at Risk*, disappointed arts educators. It mentioned arts education but did not recommend it as part of the basic curriculum.

The education crisis of the previous forty years continued into the 1990s. The dropout rate for high school students remained above 25 percent and SAT scores increased only slightly. American students had lower achievement levels than their counterparts in most other developed countries and were still functionally unprepared to maintain and help move a technological society forward. The problems persisted despite the fact that in 1990 the nation spent $215.5 billion on education, more than twice the amount it had spent ten years earlier. There was some progress in the 1990s, however. Early in that decade, the federal government renewed its involvement in education reform, which led to the most significant reform efforts since the 1950s: the enactment of federal legislation to adopt national education standards. Diane Ravitch pointed out that, before the establishment of the standards, there had never been significant agreement on what students should learn in the various subjects and at different grade levels. The national standards served as a unifying vehicle for agreement on what knowledge students throughout the country should have (Ravitch 1995).

The Federal Government

The federal government had begun to take an interest in public education even before the launch of Sputnik. The United States Office of Education (USOE), a bureau of the Department of Health, Education and Welfare, identified critical subjects that were eligible for support from the National Defense Education Act (NDEA) of 1958. Music was one of the eligible subjects.

In 1953, USOE had been transferred to the Federal Security Agency, which became the Department of Health, Education and Welfare (HEW) under President Jimmy Carter in 1980. HEW created the Arts and Humanities Branch during president John Kennedy's administration. Kathryn Bloom was Branch Chief, and Harold Arberg, Music Specialist. Together, they worked closely with the schools and professional arts organizations but did not have large amounts of money to grant.

The Elementary and Secondary Education Act of 1965 (ESEA, PL 89-10) had great significance for American education. The law authorized more than $1.3 billion to be channeled into classrooms to achieve several education goals. Music education was one of the subjects that received ESEA funding. The section of the law most significant to music education was Title I, which was prefaced: "An ACT to strengthen and improve education quality and education opportunities in the Nation's elementary and secondary schools." School districts received funds to equalize education opportunities for children of low-income families. Title I enabled millions of children to participate in music and the other arts. Many school districts hired music teachers and purchased instruments for schools in low-income areas. During fiscal 1966, approximately one-third of the 8.3 million children in the program were involved in music or art (Lehman 1968, 53). In 1973, USOE revised the terms of Title I to increase support for the improvement of basic skills, especially reading and mathematics. Music and art were usually approved for

Title I funding only if they related in some way to the development of reading, writing, or mathematics skills, and the new interpretation greatly reduced the involvement of music and art in Title I programs.

ESEA also sponsored other arts projects. In 1966, the USOE Arts and Humanities Program sponsored forty-eight research projects in music, forty-six in art, eighteen in theater and dance, four in the arts in general, and eleven in the humanities. Some of the more significant music projects were the Yale Seminar, the Juilliard Repertory Project, and the Manhattanville Music Curriculum Program.

Four arts education associations—MENC, the National Art Education Association, the American Theatre Association, and the Dance Division of the American Association for Health, Physical Education, and Recreation[1]— established the Interdisciplinary Model Programs in the Arts for Children and Teachers (IMPACT) under the Teacher Retraining Authorization of 1970. Some of the projects it funded demonstrated that core activities in the arts could transform the traditional school curriculum (Mark 1996, 95–96). IMPACT agreed with the third paragraph of the Tanglewood Declaration of 1967: "The arts afford a continuity with the aesthetic tradition in man's history. Music and other fine arts, largely non-verbal in nature, reach close to the social, psychological, and physiological roots of man in his search for identity and self realization."

The National Foundation on the Arts and the Humanities

The Foundation was created in 1965 by PL 89-209 as an independent federal agency in the executive branch. Congress declared:

> The practice of art and the study of the humanities requires constant dedication and devotion and . . . while no government can call a great artist or scholar into existence, it is necessary and appropriate for the Federal Government to help create and sustain not only a climate encouraging freedom of thought, imagination, and inquiry, but also the material conditions facilitating the release of this creative talent.

In 1983, Frank Hodsell, chairman of the National Endowment for the Arts, announced that NEA was going to become more involved with arts education. The next year, NEA held five regional meetings in cooperation with the National Assembly of State Arts Agencies:

---

1. Known as DAMT (*Dance, Art, Music, Theatre*).

To help identify and disseminate techniques, strategies and resources for promoting arts education from kindergarten through 12th grade . . . to find exemplary efforts that improve and promote arts education in schools all across the country. These efforts might be at the state, local or classroom level, and might relate to programs, school board policies or legislative mandates. (Prince and Platt 1984, memo)

New programs to bring the arts to children were instituted under the title Learning in the Arts for Children and Youth. Its funded programs took place in schools and in communities outside of the schools. Throughout its history, NEA has spent more than $260 million on arts education initiatives, including areas of policy, practice, and partnerships.

The National Alliance for Arts Education

Congress mandated that the John F. Kennedy Center for the Performing Arts, as a national symbol of excellence in the arts, become a vehicle and focal point for strengthening the arts in education at all levels. In 1973, the Kennedy Center, together with the United States Office of Education, established the Alliance for Arts Education (AAE). AAE gives young people access to the Kennedy Center as performers and as audience members. AAE is a coalition of not-for-profit statewide Alliances for Arts Education that work with the Kennedy Center to support the arts as an essential part of K–12 education. Each state alliance promotes and advocates for arts education. Several offer arts education activities in addition to advocacy.

In the spring of 1976, the organizations of the DAMT group worked with the U.S. Office of Education and the Alliance for Arts Education to conduct its arts advocacy project. Leaders from five education administration associations came to the center for a weekend of performances and discussion. Subsequently, the DAMT organizations oversaw an evaluation of all arts projects that had been granted federal funding. The report, *Try a New Face*, was published in 1979.

Federally Funded Music Education Projects

The National Science Foundation (NSF) had sponsored science curriculum development projects, which led President Kennedy to appoint the Panel on Educational Research and Development. Some of the members were concerned about the heavy emphasis on the sciences in the emerging school curriculum. Many successful scientists were accomplished musicians, and they believed that serious study of the arts and humanities would improve science education if students were exposed to a view of human experience as seen through those disciplines.

The panel recommended that the K–12 music curriculum be examined to discover why public school music programs had not produced a musically literate and active public. Yale University was granted an award by the USOE Cooperative Research Programs for a seminar on music education. Claude V. Palisca, professor of musicology at Yale University, was director of the Yale Seminar.[2]

The Yale Seminar criticized the quality of music in school music programs. It recognized the accomplishments of music educators in the area of performance. It criticized music educators because performance skill development often was used for showmanship and other superficial musical experiences rather than for the aesthetic impact of great music. The seminar pointed out that the school music program had not kept pace with twentieth century musical developments. The majority of participants were musicologists and other educators not involved with music education in the public schools, and so the seminar had little influence on music education practices.

The Juilliard Repertory Project

Shortly after the conclusion of the Yale Seminar, Dean Gideon Waldrop of the Juilliard School of Music applied to the U.S. Office of Education for a grant for Juilliard to develop a body of authentic and meaningful music to enrich the repertory available for grades K–6. The project began in July 1964 under the direction of the composer Vittorio Giannini, president of the North Carolina School of the Arts. Reminiscent of the Yale grant to an institution with no connection to music education, this award was made to the Juilliard School of Music shortly after it terminated its music education program.

The Juilliard Repertory Project brought together scholars and teachers to research and collect music of the highest quality for teaching music, which satisfied the Yale Seminar recommendation for high quality, authentic music. Despite the quality of the music in the Juilliard Repertory Library and its availability, it was not widely accepted by music educators. Music educators obviously were not seeking authentic music of high quality that represented various periods and genres for their programs.[3]

---

2. It was notable that the grant went to an institution with no connection to music education.

3. The collection might have been more successful if the project had taken place at an institution with a strong music education program.

Advocacy for Music Education

Formal advocacy efforts began when MENC appointed Joan Gaines director of its new public relations program in 1966. Her initial assignment was to prepare for the Tanglewood Symposium, to be held the following year. Gaines spread the message of music education to the public, coaching music educators in making their own public relations efforts more effective. Her print advertisements and radio and television spot announcements blanketed the country. Her work was especially critical when the worldwide economic recession in the early 1970s forced education policy makers to make difficult choices about spending scarce resources. MENC began to refocus its efforts from public relations to government relations. By the 1980s, MENC had acquired considerable expertise in advocacy, had participated in numerous legislative agendas, and had taken formal positions in diverse federal issues. Several MENC presidents have testified before Congressional committees in Washington. A 1986 briefing paper to the arts education community stated:

> Clearly, the advocacy movement is on the cultural formation scene in force. The arts education community must relate to the advocacy movement as positively as possible without giving up the intellectual ground on which the whole notion of serious education in the arts disciplines is based. (K–12 Arts Education 1989)

In 1988, MENC, the International Music Products Association, and the National Association of Recording Arts and Sciences, formed the National Coalition for Education in the Arts. Its mission was to develop and monitor policy affecting education in the arts. The coalition successfully advocated the inclusion of arts education in the Goals 2000 Act to the United States Department of Education.

Other Advocacy Efforts

Professional arts education organizations were not the only advocates for arts education. In 1979, the prestigious Arts Education and Americans Panel, chaired by David Rockefeller Jr., described the status of arts education at that time in the book *Coming to Our Senses*, which offered a warning for the future of American culture if arts education was not made more secure. Rockefeller wrote:

> If we want our world to be still, gray and silent, then we should take the arts out of school, shut down the neighborhood theatre, and barricade

the museum doors. When we let the arts into the arena of learning, we run the risk that color and motion and music will enter our lives. (Rockefeller 1979)

In 1990, MENC, the National Association of Music Merchants, and the National Academy of Recording Arts and Sciences created the National Commission on Music Education. The Commission heard testimony at public forums in Los Angeles, Chicago, and Nashville, and at a national symposium in Washington in 1991. In that year, MENC published the Commission's report, *Growing Up Complete: The Imperative for Music Education* (National Commission 1991). *Growing Up Complete* was a key element in the effort to have the arts included in the *Goals 2000* legislation. It was distributed to Congress, the White House, parent groups, arts and education organizations, major corporations, advocacy groups, and individuals concerned about the arts in education.

Of all the education projects the federal government initiated or participated in, the most significant for arts education was the national standards for arts education. The National Standards were a product of the Congressional act entitled *Goals 2000: Educate America Act* (PL 103-227), which originated in the six National Education Goals of 1990. Originally, the arts were not included with the core subjects. It was only after extensive advocacy efforts that Secretary of Education Richard Riley agreed to include them. This was MENC's most consequential, far-reaching advocacy achievement to that time. Paul Lehman described the importance of advocacy by arts education organizations:

> The standards project has given arts educators control of the agenda in the debate over arts education. It has enabled arts educators to lead the discussion. This was not the case previously. In past years, for example, initiatives in arts education were routinely taken by advocacy groups or other organizations with no competence or experience in arts education, and not surprisingly, nothing worthwhile or permanent happened. But now MENC has seized the initiative and has proven that it's a major force on the Washington scene. Don't underestimate the significance of that achievement. (1994)

The Contemporary Music Project

The Contemporary Music Project (CMP) was a major project to help the music education profession modernize itself to serve contemporary societal needs. The Ford Foundation announced its intention to improve the relationship between the arts and American society in 1957, and in 1959, it sponsored the Young Composers Project. The project placed composers not over thirty-five years of age in public school systems to serve as composers-in-residence. Twelve composers were placed during the first year of the project, and by 1962, thirty-one had participated. Students and teachers gained first-hand experience with contemporary music from their composers-in-residence and became more receptive to new music; the composers gained a better understanding of the musical needs of schools.

In 1963, the Ford Foundation awarded a grant of $1.38 million to MENC to organize the Contemporary Music Project for Creativity in Music Education (CMP). The Young Composers Project was continued as part of the CMP under the title Composers in Public Schools. The purposes of the CMP were to (1) increase the emphasis on the creative aspect of music in the public schools; (2) create a solid foundation or environment in the music education profession for the acceptance, through understanding, of the contemporary music idiom; (3) reduce the compartmentalization between music composition and music education for the benefit of composers and music educators alike; (4) cultivate taste and discrimination on the part of music educators and students regarding the quality of contemporary music used in schools; and (5) discover creative talent among students (CMP in Perspective 1973).

The CMP sponsored workshops and seminars at sixteen colleges and universities throughout the country to help teachers better understand contemporary music through analysis, performance, and pedagogy. There were six pilot projects in elementary and secondary schools to provide authentic situations for teaching contemporary music. In 1965, the Seminar on Comprehensive Musicianship was held at Northwestern University to propose ways to improve the education of music teachers, which was one of the most important functions of the CMP. The movement known as *Comprehensive Musicianship* developed from the seminar.

Composer David Ward-Steinman's approach was one of many that went beyond the traditional music curriculum. He found the traditional curriculum "limiting, confining, unnecessarily dull, and ultimately self-defeating." He favored the CMP approach because it involved students deeply in listening, composing, and performing, including improvisation. Students addressed relationships between Western classical music and other Western and non-Western musics, and the relationship between music and art. The CMP program unified the study of music by bringing together theory, harmony, ear training, counterpoint, form analysis, instrumental and arranging, and history in a two-year sequence of broad-based courses (Sullivan 1979).

The goal of the Contemporary Music Project was "to provide a synthesis, a focus, for disparate activities in music, in order to give them a cohesion and relevance in our society, to its cultural and educational institutions and organizations." It had been fulfilled when the program ended in 1973. The CMP gave direction, provided challenges, developed methodology and materials, and had made the music education profession more receptive to change and innovation (Mark 1986, 35–40).

Music Education for Adults

Roy Ernst of the Eastman School of Music established The New Horizons movement of bands, orchestras, and choruses for people aged fifty-five and older. In 1991, Ernst received a grant for the project from the National Association of Music Merchants and the International Band and Orchestral Products Association. New Horizons creates an entry point to group music making for adult beginners and a comfortable reentry point for adults who played music in school and would like to resume after long years of building careers and raising children. Ernst wrote:

> I thought that being involved in music groups would help to improve quality of life for retired people. They would enjoy the challenge and accomplishment of learning music and they would have a new group of friends with whom they shared a common interest. They would also have events to anticipate—concert, other gigs, and trips. There was also information at that time indicating that music study would support good mental and physical health. . . . The first New Horizons Band started at the Eastman School of Music in Rochester, New York, in January of 1991. We started with about forty people. The media loved the idea of older adults starting music. After five weeks, we had a nice article in the *New York Times* and that led to a very good article on the NBC Today Show. (Ernst 2006)

Ernst believes that "anyone can learn to play music at a level that will bring a sense of accomplishment and the ability to perform in a group."

As of 2006, the movement had grown to one hundred thirty New Horizons organizations with thirty more in the planning stage. The ensembles include players from the beginner's level to musicians with advanced skills, sometimes retired professional musicians. Professors, doctors, engineers, attorneys, and "just about everything else" are represented in the groups. The teachers are school music educators with experience in class instruction. Their salaries and other costs are covered by tuition, and all of the groups are self-supporting.

Ernst has successfully extended music education beyond the schools to embrace members of the community who also value the services of music teachers. The New Horizons organizations are excellent examples of cooperation between school and community music. While the musicians benefit in many ways, so do the teachers, who have the unique opportunity to expand their own professional vision.

NEW FOUNDATIONS OF MUSIC EDUCATION

Society was evolving rapidly as the 1950s ushered Americans into the technological age. As change began to affect many areas of life, it became critical that educators find ways to accommodate the curriculum to a new kind of society. Music educators, aware that they could not offer a 1930s curriculum in a time of fast and radical societal change, began to seek ways to modernize their offerings.

Music education in the 1950s was similar in content and method to music education in the 1930s. Music had been an integral part of the school curriculum during the progressive education era, and when progressive education ceased to be an organized movement in the 1950s, music, like the other curricular disciplines, lost a philosophical basis of support. Subject matter specialists were left to develop their particular areas as they saw fit.

The need to reform curricula during the late 1950s and 1960s was pressing. The emerging technological society depended on education to develop young people's ability to perceive relationships, rather than to absorb isolated fragments of knowledge. This was necessary if students were to cope with developments in all fields of knowledge. John Goodlad wrote:

> The curriculum and the students of tomorrow may be better served by subjects and subject combinations other than those deemed important today. But curriculum planning takes place in such a piecemeal fashion that across-the-board examination of the total school experience of children and youth is not likely to occur. In all probability, new accretions and formulations will occur in the traditional school subjects if the curriculum revision procedures of the past decade continue. But ongoing inquiry in fields not now firmly established in the curriculum is likely to go unnoticed unless we concentrate on the aims of schooling rather than on the organization of specific subjects. (Goodlad 1966, 14–16)

Curriculum developers looked to a conceptual approach to learning. The traditional method of imparting a body of facts to children was outdated at a time when knowledge was expanding at an ever-increasing rate. It was no longer possible to choose the body of facts that would be meaningful to students in the future. Instead, curriculum was organized by concepts, principles, and modes of inquiry, making it possible for students to know how to learn what would be important for their individual needs. The ability to think inductively to resolve unfamiliar problems became the goal of curriculum planners.

Aesthetic Education

There was a critical need for a central unifying philosophy of music education. Several books and events paved the way for the development of a new philosophy that came to be known as aesthetic education. The early leaders in this movement were Charles Leohnard, of the University of Illinois, and Allan Britton, of the University of Michigan. They called for an intellectual grounding for the profession that did not rely on ancillary, or utilitarian, values but rather on students' depth of understanding of music itself. They pointed out that although music might be good for children in any number of ways (such as improved behavior or health, for example), other school subjects could bring about the same improvements, often more effectively than music. They emphasized that it was the music that made music education unique among school subjects.

Britton and Leonhard advocated that the philosophical discipline of aesthetics should be the basis of the new philosophy of music education. They held that the beliefs of several philosophers demonstrated consonance between aesthetics and music education. The writings of John Dewey, Leonard Meyer, and Susanne Langer were to be the foundation of the new philosophy. Langer's books, *Philosophy in a New Key* and *Feeling and Form,* and Meyer's book, *Emotion and Meaning Music,* were integral to the emerging philosophy because they established an intrinsic connection between music and emotion. The central point was their recognition of music, specifically Western art music, as being expressive of feeling. This was especially critical in the new technological age, when people feared that individualism was being repressed by the newly emerging technological society. The need for individual emotional development and growth was to provide a balance to the new emphasis on science, mathematics, and engineering.

MENC established its Commission on Basic Concepts in 1954, which persuaded the National Society for the Study of Education to devote its

1958 yearbook to music education. Distinguished authors in disciplines related to music education contributed chapters to the yearbook, entitled *Basic Concepts in Music Education. Basic Concepts* was the first attempt to publish guidelines for the development of a profession-wide philosophy of music education. Allen Britton cited historical justification for music education and advocated the use of music in schools for its own sake, rather than for ancillary or utilitarian benefits.

> Music, as one of the seven liberal arts, has formed an integral art of the educational systems of Western civilization from Hellenic times to the present. Thus, the position of music in education historically speaking, is one of great strength. Unfortunately, this fact seems to be one of which most educators, including music educators, remain unaware. As a result, the defense of music in the curriculum is often approached as if something new were being dealt with. Lacking the assurance which a knowledge of history could provide, many who seek to justify the present place of music in American schools tend to place too heavy a reliance upon ancillary values which music may certainly serve but which cannot, in the end, constitute its justification. Plato, of course, is the original offender in this regard, and his general view that the essential value of music lies in its social usefulness seems to be as alive today as ever. (Britton 1958, 195)

In 1959, another book that was significant for music education philosophy was published—*Foundations and Principles of Music Education* by Charles Leonhard and Robert House.

The two books articulated a foundational belief in the value of music education that set the stage for the development of the philosophy of music as aesthetic education. They presented new philosophical, sociological, psychological, and historical views of music education, and together they established the profession's agenda for future intellectual developments. The books were widely adopted. Charles Leonhard wrote:

> When we speak of a philosophy of music education, we refer to a system of basic beliefs which underlies and provides a basis for the operation of the musical enterprise in an educational setting. . . . The business of the school is to help young people undergo meaningful experience and arrive at a system of values that will be beneficial to society. . . . While reliance on statements of the instrumental value of music may well have convinced some reluctant administrator more fully to support the music program, those values cannot stand close scrutiny, because they are not directly related to music and are not unique to music. In fact, many

other areas of the curriculum are in a position to make a more powerful contribution to these values than is music. (Leonhard 1965, 42–43)

Music educators were to teach music for its own value to enrich the lives of their students.

Bennett Reimer described the evolution toward aesthetic education:

If music education in the present era could be characterized by a single, overriding purpose, one would have to say this field is trying to become "aesthetic education." What is needed in order to fulfill this purpose is a philosophy which shows how and why music education is aesthetic in its nature and its value. (Reimer 1970, 2)

The philosophy of music education as aesthetic education was moved forward when Charles Leonhard invited one of his graduate students, Bennett Reimer, to write a book on music education philosophy. The book was *A Philosophy of Music Education*. Reimer wrote:

The profession as a whole needs a formulation which can serve to guide the efforts of the group. The impact the profession can make on society depends in large degree on the quality of the profession's understanding of what it has to offer which might be of value to society. There is an almost desperate need for a better understanding of the value of music and of the teaching and learning of music. . . . The tremendous expenditure of concern about how to justify itself—both to itself and to others—which has been traditional in this field, reflects a lack of philosophical "inner peace." (Reimer 1970, 3)

Seeking music education's "inner peace," he articulated an intellectual basis for the profession that still serves as the belief system for many music educators. Aesthetic education influenced school curricula and served as a focal point for those who thought about the value of music in education. Reimer's approach to music education philosophy was through the music itself. It was consonant with conceptual learning, the process that had recently been accepted by American schools.

Although aesthetic education permeated music education in the 1960s and 1970s, concerns began to emerge about its suitability for non-Western musics, especially after the Tanglewood Declaration had given its blessing to the use of musics of all cultures in school programs. Abraham Schwadron, who had strongly supported aesthetic education, "straddled the line in his writings between the need for the professional security that might be achieved through a unified philosophy and the realities of a pluralistic society" (McCarthy and Goble 2002). Schwadron's research in the fields of musicology, anthropology, and religion gave him a broad view of the purpose of music education, and he advocated for a philosophy that could embrace "socio-musical values and related educational means and ends" (Schwadron 1967). Schwadron, along with others, became concerned that aesthetic education was not sufficiently broad and encompassing to serve the needs of a multi-cultural society.

As music educators debated their philosophical beliefs and concerns, a new philosophy, praxialism[4] emerged (Elliott 1994). David Elliott, a former student of Reimer, led in the development of a divergent view that emphasized musical participation, rather than listening. He advanced Schwadron's argument, stating that aesthetic education was limited to Western art music and did not accommodate non-Western musics. Praxialism gained widespread acceptance as more music educators became interested in philosophy.

New venues for philosophical writings and debates developed. MENC established its Philosophy Special Research Interest Group in 1990. In that same year, Indiana University hosted an international symposium on the subject and in 1993 the university launched the journal *Philosophy of Music Education Review*. In 1993, the MayDay Group was established independent of MENC as a forum for the exchange of ideas. Philosophers gravitated to the MayDay Group, which quickly focused on the aesthetic education/praxial dichotomy. Philip Alperson edited the anthology *What Is Music? An Introduction to the Philosophy of Music.* The strongest voice for a praxial philosophy, however, was David Elliott's *Music Matters: A New Philosophy of Music Education. Music Matters* defined praxialism just as Reimer's *A Philosophy of Music Education* had defined aesthetic education twenty-one years earlier.

Elliott maintained that all cultures participate in what he called "a diverse human practice," which he named "MUSIC," and the people who made music, or practiced "musicing," he called "musicers." He maintained that the practice of musicing engages one in "flow experiences," so called by psychologist Mihalyi Csikszentmihalyi. Csikszentmihalyi defined flow as complete absorption, or enjoyment, of an activity as a result of deep concentration on the activity.

Philosophical discussions were not limited to the aesthetic/praxial dichotomy. Philosophers posed new topics. Estelle Jorgensen wrote *In Search of Music Education*, in which she addressed a variety of topics having to do with problems facing the profession and the role of music in sociocultural

4. From Aristotle's concept of *praxis,* or action originating in practice, rather than in theory.

communities. Other philosophers, including Thomas Regelski, Wayne Bowman, John Blacking, Mary Reichling, Julia Koza, Marja Heimonen, and Keith Swanick, also contributed books and articles on topics of current interest to philosophers.

Psychology and Music Education

At the same time that aesthetic education was beginning to influence music education philosophy, conceptual education, a new view of how children learn, emerged. Conceptual education directly influenced the music curriculum. Before the 1960s, teachers used a variety of approaches to rote learning that required children to memorize specific information. Educators believed that children understood a subject after learning its basic factual content. Jerome Bruner's book, *The Process of Education* (Bruner 1960), established an important basis for curriculum development in all subject areas and influenced instructional practices. *The Process of Education* articulated four themes: the role of structure in learning and how it can be made central in teaching; readiness for learning; intuition; and how the desire to learn can be stimulated. The impact of Bruner's work on curriculum development was profound. Music educators studied the implications of conceptual learning, formulated new ideas about teaching and learning music, and developed new practices and curricular materials. Russell Getz described the influence of conceptual learning on music education:

> One of the greatest changes for better music teaching was the gradual acceptance by general music teachers of the concept approach, as compared to previous efforts, which were often more concerned with associative properties of music. Instead of emphasizing story-telling through program music and correlating music with geography, social studies, mathematics, and science, the heart of music education has become the study of music itself, the components of pitch, duration, dynamics, and timbre, and the resultant concomitants such as melody, harmony, rhythm, instrumentation, style, and form. (Getz 1984, 24–25)

One of the most important publications to relate conceptual learning practices to music education was *The Study of Music in the Elementary School—A Conceptual Approach* (Gary 1967). The book offered ideas to assist children in developing musical concepts that would permit them to discover the structure and meaning of musical works. It presented information about concepts such as rhythm, melody, harmony, form in music, tempo, dynamics, and tone color.

Connectionism

Connectionism (also known as associationism) was one of the early influential schools of thought in the philosophy of education. A leading connectionist, Edward L. Thorndike, held that learning establishes bonds between specific stimuli and responses and does not result from strengthening the faculties by conquering difficult challenges (Thorndike 1918, 16). This principal worked well for small bits of learning and became the basis for the teaching machines of computer-assisted instruction.

Testing

Carl E. Seashore's *Measures of Musical Talents* was first published in 1919. Interest in aptitude testing remained strong for at least seventy years after the first Seashore tests appeared. He revised the *Measures* in 1938, and used a composite score rather than evaluating responses separately for each musical element, but he did not change the basic structure of the tests.

James L. Mursell

Mursell was a member of the distinguished faculty at Columbia University Teachers College. He served on the editorial board of the *Music Supervisors Journal,* was a member of the MSNC Research Council, and produced voluminous writings in books and periodicals. Mursell guided the thinking of many music educators throughout the middle third of the twentieth century.

Edwin Gordon

Edwin Gordon recognized the importance of authentic musical experience during the pre-school years as a means of raising potential musical aptitude, which he said were unchangeable after about the age of ten. His *Musical Aptitude Profile* (Gordon 1971) required students to record progress on a weekly basis.

Four Schools of Psychology

Several schools of psychology related to music education evolved during the second half of the twentieth century: behaviorism, cognitivism, humanism, and what Rideout calls "a socio-biological model to which no label has yet been applied" (Rideout 2002).

The behaviorist school was advanced by psychologist B. F. Skinner of Harvard University. Behaviorists theorized that learning was to be reinforced by external motivation such as recognition for achievement, or prizes like contest medals, or other kinds of motivational rewards. Behaviorism utilized behavioral objectives, which allowed for assessment based on demonstrated actions.

Followers of the cognitive approach believe that children need guided activities matched to their level of maturity. Humanism, especially in connection with the work of psychologist Abraham Maslow, related the study of the arts to the highest level of psychological achievement. Maslow called this level "self-actualization." The sociobiological model is embraced by psychologists who study how music activities relate to higher academic achievement and possibly even increased intelligence. The most famous research in this area, known as the "Mozart effect," was accomplished by Frances Rauscher. Other researchers delved even deeper into biological changes of the brain brought about by participation in music to discover whether the biological foundation of the brain can be altered through exposure to music.

An Expanding View of the Music Education Profession

A particularly revealing event of the late 1960s and 1970s about how music education had expanded was the publication by Prentice-Hall of a series of books edited by Charles Leonhard: *Contemporary Perspectives in Music Education*. One of Leonhard's colleagues, Marilyn Pflederer Zimmerman, was an expert in the theories of Piaget, and several of his doctoral students were writing dissertations on psychologists like Robert Gagne and Jerome Bruner. Leonhard invited several of his students and other researchers and scholars to contribute books on particular topics. The series reflected the interests and needs of the music education profession in 1970, at least in the mind of Charles Leonhard, one of its most knowledgeable leaders. The titles indicate how far the profession had progressed by that time:

Edwin Gordon: *The Psychology of Music Teaching* (1971)
Robert Klotman: *The School Music Administrator and Supervisor: Catalysts for Change in Music Education* (1973)
Richard Colwell: *The Evaluation of Music Teaching and Learning* (1970)
Clifford Madsen and Charles Madsen: *Experimental Research in Music* (1970)
Paul Lehman: *Tests and Measurements in Music* (1968)
Bennett Reimer: *A Philosophy of Music Education* (1970)

Robert Sidnell: *Building Instructional Programs in Music Education Psychology* (1973)

Music Education and Multiculturalism

When the United States entered World War II in 1941, a new drive for unity among the United States and the Latin American nations influenced music education. Musicologist Charles Seeger and MENC Associate Executive Secretary Vanett Lawler helped establish the Advisory Council on Music Education in the Latin American Republics. The *Music Educators Journal* published articles on Latin American folk music, and MENC conferences featured sessions on the subject.

By the second half of the century, colleges and universities had broadened their musicology programs to extend beyond the traditional Eurocentric vision of music. The Society for Ethnomusicology and the International Society for Music Education were founded in 1953. Musicologists became interested in African and Asian musics, and their new interest influenced music education. Patricia Shehan Campbell wrote:

> The music of Africa and Asia came trickling into textbooks of the 1950s and 1960s as transcriptions of recordings or re-makes of missionary and military collections, complete with full piano scores. The internationalization of the music curriculum was sputtering along, with elementary music teachers increasingly taking and translating for their needs the music of the world into suitable forms for the performance by their young students. (Campbell 2002, 30–31)

The civil rights movement gained momentum at this time, fueled by the victory of the 1954 Supreme Court *Brown v. Board of Education* decision. That momentous action desegregated America's public schools, although it did not actually integrate them. The *Brown* decision had little immediate impact on music education but eventually music teachers began to incorporate ethnic musics, jazz, and what came to be known as "youth music," in recognition of the culture of American youth. It was a decade before the music education profession officially acknowledged that schools with large minority populations needed music programs designed to meet the particular needs of urban students. The Tanglewood Symposium of 1967 brought official recognition that music of all kinds and styles had a legitimate place in the curriculum.

One of the goals of the Goals and Objectives (GO) Project of 1968–1969 was to investigate the "musics of non-Western cultures and their uses in education." In October 1972, MENC published a special interest edition of the *Music Educators Journal* that featured musics of world cultures. In 1972, James Standifer and Barbara Reeder Lundquist published their *Source Book of African and Afro-American Materials for Music Educators*, and MENC created the National Black Music Caucus in that year.

The expansion of multicultural musics in the curriculum has continued since that time. Professional development materials and activities have been offered in MENC conference programs and publications, and from organizations like the American Orff-Schulwerk Association, the American Choral Directors Association, and the Organization of Kodály Educators. The International Society for Music Education has provided a rich offering of multicultural musics to music educators from many nations. The MENC multicultural community expanded in 2006, when it established a new membership classification for Mariachi educators. This step advanced MENC's mission of "Music for All."

New Approaches to Curriculum

New music curricula were introduced in the late 1950s and 1960s. Several were imported from other countries, where they had already proven their success. They fit well into American education because they were compatible with the new conceptual learning movement.

Eurhythmics or the Dalcroze Method

Eurhythmics was based on the work of Emile Jaques-Dalcroze (1865–1950), a Swiss musician who stressed the importance of training the musical faculties, as opposed to the common practice of teaching technique but not musicality. Dalcroze was one of the first musicians to delve into the new science of psychology. He studied with his friend, the psychologist Edouard Clarapede, who recognized the potential of the Dalcroze method for teaching children. Mabelle Glenn derived her graded series, *World of Music,* from Dalcroze eurhythmics, which was introduced in the United States early in the twentieth century. The Dalcroze method emphasized tone and rhythm, using movement to express musical interpretation. Dalcroze wrote:

> It is true that I first devised my method as a musician for musicians. But the further I carried my experiments, the more I noticed that, while a method intended to develop the sense for rhythm, and indeed based on such development, is of great importance in the education of a musician, its chief value lies in the fact that it trains the powers of apperception and

of expression in the individual and renders easier the externalization of natural emotions. Experience teaches me that a man is not ready for the specialized study of an art until his character is formed, and his powers of expression developed. (Sadler 1915, 32)

Although the Dalcroze method has not been adopted into the American music curriculum, its philosophy and many of its techniques have been incorporated into other methods. Many American teachers have studied it. An example is the use of walking and running as designations for quarter and eighth notes (Hoffer 1983, 123). By the 1930s, many college music schools and physical education departments required courses in *eurhythmics*, the term for Dalcroze-like instruction.

The Orff Approach

The approach of Carl Orff (1895–1982) was based on his interest in folk music, nineteenth century popular song, dance and theatre music, and medieval, baroque, and Renaissance music. The dance movement theories of Emile Jaques-Dalcroze intrigued Orff and in 1924 he and the dancer Dorothea Gunther founded the Gunther Schule. The school was an innovative ensemble of dancers and musicians who trained teachers in new forms of movement and rhythm. Improvisation was a major part of the program. Many of the students were preparing to be physical education teachers. Assisted by Curt Sachs and Karl Maendler, Orff developed an instrumental ensemble at the Gunther Schule, which Orff described as follows:

> In due course the Gunther school boasted an ensemble of dancers with an orchestra of their own. Music and choreography were supervised by Gunild Keetman and Maja Lex, respectively. Dancers and players were interchangeable. Suitable instruments (flutes, cymbals, drums, etc.) were integrated into the dance itself. The diverse and varied instruments employed included recorders, xylophones, and metallophones of all ranges, glockenspiels, kettledrums, small drums, tomtoms, gongs, various kinds of cymbals, triangles, tone bells; and sometimes also fiddles, gambas, spinettinos, and portatives. (Landis and Carder 1972, 156)

The ensemble played for education conferences and teachers meetings throughout Germany. World War II interrupted plans to test the Orff-Gunther approach on a larger scale in German schools, and the Gunther Schule was destroyed during the war. After the war, a Bavarian radio official discovered an out-of-print recording from the Gunther Schule. His interest in the recording led to the gradual rekindling of national interest in Orff's work. When Orff reflected on the method that he had developed before the war, he considered that rhythm education might be more effective with young children than with adults. He concluded that elemental (primeval or basic) music evolving from speech, movement, and dance could become the basis of early childhood music education. He and his lifelong associate Gunild Keetman began to test the idea in nursery schools and kindergartens.

A radio broadcast series in 1948 of children performing elemental music on a small set of Orff instruments brought widespread interest in music for children. Between 1950 and 1954, Orff published his five volume *Music for Children*, a compilation and complete reworking of the prewar work. The method, *Schulwerk*, attracted international interest. The books were translated into eighteen languages and the exercises were adapted to the native rhythms and music of the countries that imported Orff's techniques. The Canadian adaptation[5] by Doreen Hall and Arnold Walter consists of five volumes and a teacher's edition. It corresponds to the original Schulwerk in progression of subject matter, but the music was selected or written especially for English-speaking children.

The Orff approach was adopted in private and public schools throughout the United States. The American Orff Schulwerk Association was founded in 1963 at Ball State University to disseminate information about Schulwerk in the United States through its publication, *the Orff Echo*, and through workshops.

The Kodály Method

Hungarian composer Zoltan Kodály (1882–1967) was concerned that twentieth century Hungarian life was less musical than it had been in the nineteenth century. Hungarian society no longer stimulated musicality in individuals and Kodály believed that it was the responsibility of the schools to remedy the situation. He created a pedagogical system to help the schools reawaken the Hungarian peoples' musicality. Kodály's method grew from his belief that Hungarian music education should teach the spirit of singing to everyone and to educate all to be musically literate. He wanted to bring music into everyday use in homes and in leisure activities, and to educate concert audiences.

Kodály was concerned with the creative, humanizing enrichment of life through music. Universal music literacy was the first step toward his

---

5. This is the edition used in the United States.

ideal (Edwards 1971). He also wanted to build a national music culture through his approach to teaching music in the schools, using nationalistic and folk songs. Kodály's method was adapted for use in the United States by Tibor Bachmann, Lois Choksy, Mary Helen Richards, and Denise Bacon. American music educators learned the method from writings, workshops, and a variety of programs offered by colleges and specialized schools. Many studied in Hungary. The Organization of American Kodály Educators (OAKE) was formed in 1974 to support and promote Kodály education in the United States. Its official journal is *The Kodály Envoy*. OAKE became an associated organization of MENC in 1984.

The Suzuki Method

The method of Sinichi Suzuki (1898–1998) was another imported curriculum that influenced American music education. Suzuki was born in Japan, the son of the first Japanese commercial violin manufacturer. He learned about violin design and construction while working in his father's factory. Suzuki's musical training began in Japan, and later he studied for eight years with Karl Klinger in Berlin.

Suzuki adopted a young orphaned boy in Matsumoto and taught him to play the violin. His success encouraged him to create *Talent Education*, which he called the "mother tongue method." It is based on psycholinguistic development. Children learn their native language easily and naturally, while adults learn languages only with great difficulty. Suzuki recognized the potential of young children to learn much more than is normally expected of them. He believed that if children have the ability to learn something as challenging as language, the same ability must also allow them to master other kinds of knowledge and skills the way they learn their mother tongue. Observation, imitation, and repetition are the key to gradual development of intellectual awareness.

American string teachers were introduced to Talent Education in 1958, when they viewed a film of 750 Japanese children playing the Bach *Concerto for Two Violins*. The film was presented at a meeting of the American String Teachers Association at Oberlin College. The teachers were so impressed that they sent John Kendall to observe Suzuki's method. Kendall traveled to Japan in 1959 and again in 1962 to continue his study.

In 1964, Suzuki traveled to the United States with ten children who performed at several locations and at the Music Educators National Conference convention in Philadelphia. The performance was a revelation to the American teachers, who saw for the first time that four- and five-year-old

Japanese children were able to play professional level music, while American children usually did not begin to study the violin at such a young age.

Talent Education grew in the United States after the 1964 convention. American string educators John Kendall, Paul Rolland, and Tibor Zelig solved problems that arose in adapting the method for American children and developed their own successful Suzuki programs. Since then, Suzuki programs have found their way into some public schools, and numerous private Talent Education schools operate throughout the country.

Comprehensive Musicianship

Comprehensive Musicianship was an American development to improve the music curriculum by integrating aspects of music usually studied separately as discrete subjects. Music history, theory, performance, and conducting were often taught as separate subjects, making it difficult for students to relate them to each other. The integrated study of music prevented the fragmentation of musical knowledge and understanding.

The Contemporary Music Project (CMP) was the catalyst for comprehensive musicianship. In 1965, CMP sponsored the "Seminar on Comprehensive Musicianship—the Foundation for College Education in Music" at Northwestern University. The participants, including scholars, educators, theorists, composers, historians, and performers examined the content and orientation of basic college music courses in history and theory. The seminar generated Institutes for Music in Contemporary Education (IMCE) at six universities to implement comprehensive musicianship. Relatively few colleges instituted comprehensive musicianship programs. It had more influence in elementary and secondary schools, where most performance ensembles did not have a formal curriculum. The music itself was the curriculum. R. Jack Mercer described the problem:

> There are few band curricula that take the student through the basics of music theory and history. Instead, scores are selected to meet the requirements of the next performance, and the curriculum is the score. Consequently, the content of the course of study is fortuitous, depending almost entirely upon whether it is football season or concert season. . . . The goal of musical training is to present a polished musical performance. (Mercer 1972, 51–53)

The solution to the problem was in the music used by performing ensembles. It was the basis for musical learning analysis, theory, and historical information. This approach required a great deal of preparation by directors, and rehearsals became combinations of rehearsal, class, and laboratory. Comprehensive musicianship was also applied to general music classes, where the curriculum often had been based on a unit approach that addressed extramusical topics like the lives of composers.

The Hawaii Music Curriculum Program

The Hawaii program began in 1968 under the sponsorship of the Hawaii Curriculum Center in Honolulu. It was established "to create a logical, continuous educational program ensuring the competent guidance of the music education of all children in the state's public schools and to test and assemble the materials needed by schools to realize this program" (Thomson 1970, 73). It was designed to implement comprehensive musicianship concepts and practices in the public school music program. The term *comprehensive* meant that students were to be involved with music in school in the same ways that people are involved with it in the outside world because the school should be a microcosm of the outside world. The book *Comprehensive Musicianship through Classroom Music* (Thompson 1974) resulted from the Hawaii Music Curriculum Program.

The Manhattanville Music Curriculum Program

The Manhattanville Music Curriculum Program (MMCP) was influential in implementing comprehensive musicianship in school music programs. The premise of the Manhattanville curriculum was summarized in 1970 by its creator, Ronald Thomas:

> If music is an expressive medium, learning involves expressing. If it is a creative art, learning means creating. If music has meaning, personal judgments are fundamental to the learning process. If music is a communicative art, the educational process must involve students in communication. Facts may be taught, but meaning is discovered. There is nothing antecedent to discovering meaning. (Thomas 1970, 70)

The premise of MMCP was that learning is based on a spiral curriculum, a reflection of Jerome Bruner's theory of learning. MMCP was funded by a grant from the United States Office of Education and was named for Manhattanville College, where it originated. Its objective was to develop a music curriculum and related materials for a sequential music learning program for the primary grades through high school. MMCP was used in some schools, but the most common usage was the adaptation of its concepts and strategies for traditional music programs.

The Civil Rights Movement

Changes in American society in the 1960s persuaded many educators that the popular arts have a legitimate place in American education. The massive 1960s demonstrations and protests and the civil rights movement brought many changes to American culture, one of which was increased permissiveness toward the younger generation and acceptance of its taste in clothing, music, and other lifestyle characteristics. Colleges that had not recognized the popular arts earlier began to develop degree programs in jazz. Secondary schools that had offered elective courses only in music appreciation created special interest courses in jazz, rock, and ethnic musics.

The Tanglewood Symposium recognized the value of all kinds of music, and promoted the use of popular musics in the curriculum. The symposium participants agreed that it is not possible or appropriate to recognize a hierarchy of kinds of music: "The music repertory should be expanded to involve music of our time in its rich rarity, including currently popular teenage music." This opened the way for an infusion of popular music in the curriculum, and many music educators began to adjust their programs to include it.

The National Association of Jazz Educators

The National Association of Jazz Educators (NAJE), which later became the International Association of Jazz Educators (IAJE), was immediately accepted as an associated organization of MENC upon its establishment in 1968. Its founders were Stan Kenton, Louis Wersen, John Roberts, and Charles Gary, all of whom had participated in the Tanglewood Symposium. The MENC affiliation was all but inevitable because the purpose of NAJE, "to further the understanding and appreciation of jazz and popular music, and to promote its artistic performance," was integral to the Tanglewood recommendations (Roberts 1969, 44–46). IAJE ceased to exist in 2008.

Rock was also brought into the schools, but music teachers were less familiar with it than with jazz. The Youth Music Institute was held at the University of Wisconsin in the summer of 1969 to bring together rock-oriented young people and music teachers. It was organized by Emmett Sarig, a participant in the Tanglewood Symposium, and sponsored by MENC, the U.S. Office of Education, and the Extension Music Department of the University of Wisconsin. The institute helped many music educators become more knowledgeable about the youth culture and rock music. David McAllister summarized the movement toward popular musics:

> We affirm that it is our duty to seek true musical communication with the great masses of our population. While we continue to develop and make available, to all who are interested, the great musics of the middle class and aristocracy, we must also learn the language of the great musical arts which we have labeled "base" because they are popular. . . . When we have learned that any musical expression is "music, " we hope to be able to reduce the class barriers in our schools and our concert halls. The resulting enrichment of our music will, we hope, give it a new vitality at all levels, and provide a united voice that can speak, without shame, of our democratic ideals. (McAllister 1968, 138)

TOPICS FOR THOUGHT AND DISCUSSION

1. In what ways did societal events affect music education in the late 1950s and early 1960s?
2. What influence did federal funding have on music education?
3. Why were new curricula imported from other countries rather than being invented in the United States?
4. Discuss the ways in which the Contemporary Music Project influenced music education?
5. Discuss the value of music educators becoming involved in adult education, as in the New Horizons movement.
6. In what ways did the conceptual approach to learning change music instruction?
7. Discuss the role of the philosophy of aesthetic education in music education.
8. Discuss the differences between the philosophies of aesthetic education and praxialism.
9. How might music education have developed during the second half of the twentieth century if there had not been any government involvement in education?

REFERENCES

Alperson, Philip, ed. 1994. *What Is Music? An Introduction to the Philosophy of Music.* University Park: Pennsylvania State University Press.

American Association of School Administrators. 1959. *Official Report for the Year 1958; including a Record of the Annual Meeting and Work conference on "Education and the Creative Arts."* Washington, DC: American Association of School Administrators.

Arts, Education, and Americans Panel. 1977. *Coming to Our Senses.* New York: McGraw-Hill.

Banks, J. A. 1994. "Multicultural Education: Historical Development, Dimensions, and Practice." In *Handbook of Research on Multicultural Education,* ed. J. A. Banks and C. A. McGee Banks. New York: Macmillan Publishing.

Boyle, J. David, and Robert Lathrop. 1973. "The IMPACT Experience: An Evaluation." *Music Educators Journal* 59.

Britton, Allen P. 1958. "Music in Early American Public Education: A Historical Critique." In *Basic Concepts in Music Education,* ed. N. B. Henry. Chicago: University of Chicago Press.

———. 1969. "Music: A New Start." *Britannica Review of American Education.* Vol. 1. Chicago: Encyclopedia Britannica.

Bruner, Jerome S. 1960. *The Process of Education.* Cambridge, MA: Harvard University Press.

Campbell, Patricia Shehan. 1994. "Musica Exotica, Multiculturalism, and School Music." *The Quarterly Journal of Music Teaching and Learning* 5 (2): 65–75.

———. 1996. "Music Education, and Community in a Multicultural Society." In *Cross Currents,* ed. Marie McCarthy. College Park, MD: University of Maryland.

———. 2002. "Music Education in a Time of Cultural Transformation." *Music Educators Journal* 89 (1).

Choate, R. A., ed. 1968. *Documentary Report of the Tanglewood Symposium.* Washington, DC: MENC.

"CMP in Perspective." May 1973. *Music Educators Journal* 59: 34.

Comprehensive Musicianship: The Foundation for College Education in Music. 1965. Washington, DC: Music Educators National Conference.

Conant, James B. 1959. *The American High School Today.* New York: McGraw-Hill.

Csikzentmihalyi, Mihaly. 1991. *Flow: The Psychology of Optimal Experience.* New York: HarperPerennial.

Education for All American Youth. 1944. Washington, DC: National Education Association.

Edwards, Lorraine. 1971. "The Great Animating Stream of Music." *Music Educators Journal* 57 (February).

Elliott, David. 1994. *Music Matters: A New Philosophy of Music Education.* New York: Oxford University Press.

Ernst, Roy. 2006. E-mail to Michael Mark, July 21, 2006.

Fowler, Charles. 1988. *Can We Rescue the Arts for America's Children? Coming to Our Senses Ten Years Later.* New York: American Council on the Arts.

Gary, Charles L., ed. 1967. *The Study of Music in the Elementary School: A Conceptual Approach.* Washington, DC: MENC.

Getz, Russell P. 1984."Music Education in Tomorrow's Schools: A Practical Approach." In *The Future of Music Education in America.* Rochester, NY: Eastman School of Music Press.

Goodlad, John, et al. 1966. *The Changing School Curriculum.* New York: Fund for the Advancement of Education.

Gordon, Edwin E. 1965. *Music Aptitude Profile.* Boston, MA: Houghton-Mifflin.

———. 1971. *The Psychology of Music Teaching.* Englewood Cliffs, NJ: Prentice Hall.

Henry, Nelson B., ed. 1958. *Basic Concepts in Music Education.* Fifty-seventh Yearbook of the National Society for the Study of Education, Pt. 1. Chicago: University of Chicago Press.

Hoffer, Charles R. 1983. *Introduction to Music Education.* Belmont, CA: Wadsworth.

Housewright, Wiley L. 1969. "Youth Music in Education." *Music Educators Journal* 56 (3).

Jorgensen, Estelle. 1997. *In Search of Music Education.* Urbana, IL: University of Illinois Press.

K–12 Arts Education in the United States: Present Context, Future Needs; a Briefing Paper for the Arts Education Community. 1989. Presented for discussion and comment by Music Educators National Conference, National Art Education Association, National Dance Association, National Association of Schools of Music, National Association of Schools of Art and Design, National Association of Schools of Theatre, National Association of Schools of Dance.

Landis, Beth, and Polly Carder. 1972. *The Eclectic Curriculum in American Music Education: Contributions of Dalcroze, Kodàly, and Orff.* Washington: Music Educators National Conference.

Langer, Susanne. 1942. *Philosophy in a New Key: A Study in the Symbolism of Reason, Rite, and Art.* Cambridge, MA: Harvard University Press.

———. 1953. *Feeling and Form.* New York: Charles Scribner's Sons.

Lehman, Paul R. 1968. "The National Standards: From Vision to Reality." *Music Educators Journal* 58 (2): special insert.

———. 1994. "The National Standards: From Vision to Reality." *Music Educators Journal* 58 (2): special insert.

Leonhard, Charles. 1965. "The Philosophy of Music Education—Present and Future." In *Comprehensive Musicianship: The Foundation for College Education in Music.* Washington: Music Educators National Conference.

Lowens, Irving. 1971. "MUSIC: Juilliard Repertory Project and the Schools." Washington, DC.

Mark, Michael L. 1986. *Contemporary Music Education.* 2nd ed. New York: Schirmer.

———. 2002. *Music Education: Source Readings from Ancient Greece to Today*. 3rd ed. New York: Routledge.

———. 1996. *Contemporary Music Education*. 3rd ed. New York: Schirmer.

McAllister, David. 1968. "Curriculum Must Assume a Place at the Center of Music." *Documentary Report of the Tanglewood Symposium*. Washington, DC: Music Educators National Conference.

McCarthy, M. 1993. "The Birth of Internationalism in Music Education, 1899–1938." *International Journal of Music Education* 21.

McCarthy, M., and J. Scott Goble. September 2002. "Music Education Philosophy: Changing Times." *Music Educators Journal* 89 (1).

McLaughlin, John T., ed. 1988. *Toward a New Era in Arts Education*. New York: American Council for the Arts.

Mercer, Jack. February 1972. "Is the Curriculum the Score—or More?" *Music Educators Journal* 57.

Meyer, Leonard B. 1956. *Emotion and Meaning in Music*. Chicago: University of Chicago Press.

National Commission on Music Education. 1991. *Growing Up Complete: The Imperative for Music Education*. Reston, VA: Music Educators National Conference.

Prince, Joe N., and Geoffrey Platt. 1964. Memorandum to members of Alliance for Arts Education, April 18.

Ravitch, Diane. 1995. *National Standards in American Education: A Citizen's Guide*. Washington, DC: Brookings.

Reimer, Bennett. 1970. *A Philosophy of Music Education*. Englewood Cliffs, NJ: Prentice-Hall.

Rickover, Hyman. 1959. "Book Attacks Schools." *New York Times*.

Rideout, Roger E. 2002. "Psychology and Music Education since 1950." *Music Educators Journal* 89 (1).

Roberts, John T. 1969. "MENC's Associated Organizations: NAJE." *Music Educators Journal* 55 (February).

Rockefeller, David, Jr. 1979. *Coming to Our Senses: The Significance of the Arts for American Education*. The Arts, Education and Americans Panel. New York: McGraw-Hill.

Sadler, M. E. 1915. In Emile Jaques-Dalcroze, *The Eurhythmics*. Boston: Maynard.

Sand, Ole. 1963. "Current Trends in Curriculum Planning." *Music Educators Journal*.

Schwadron, Abraham A. 1967. *Aesthetics: Dimensions for Music Education*. Reston, VA: Music Educators National Conference.

Sullivan, William. 1979. "On Education: San Diego State Goes Comprehensive." *High Fidelity/Musical America*.

Thomas, Ronald B. 1970. "Rethinking the Curriculum." *Music Educators Journal* 56 (February).

Thomson, William. May 1970. "Music Rides a Wave of Reform in Hawaii." *Music Educators Journal* 56.

————. 1974. *Comprehensive Musicianship through Classroom Music.* Belmont, CA: Addison-Wesley.

Thorndike, Edward L. 1918. "The Nature, Purposes and General Methods of Measurement of Educational Products." In *Seventeenth Yearbook*, National Society for the Study of Education. Bloomington, IL: Public School Publishing Co..

Volk, T. M. 1998. *Music, Education, and Multiculturalism.* New York: Oxford University Press.

6

MUSIC EDUCATION IN THE TWENTY-FIRST CENTURY

VISION 2020: THE HOUSEWRIGHT SYMPOSIUM ON THE FUTURE OF MUSIC EDUCATION

The twenty-first century began with a reflective event that preceded the new century by one year. It was intended to articulate an ideal vision of music education for the next two decades. Vision 2020: The Housewright Symposium on the Future of Music Education was cosponsored in 1999 by MENC, the National Association for Music Education, and the School of Music of Florida State University. MENC President June Hinckley conceived and directed the event that was reminiscent of the Tanglewood Symposium of thirty-two years earlier. As American society progressed and evolved, she felt it necessary to review the status of music education and to lay the groundwork for the profession in the near future. The title, Vision 2020, describes both the visionary nature of the event and the time period that was targeted. The name of the symposium honored Wiley Housewright, president of MENC from 1968 to 1979. Housewright led the implementation of the Tanglewood recommendations. He was dean of the School of Music of Florida State University, which hosted Vision 2020. More than 150 music educators and representatives from industry and the community attended. The symposium culminated in the Housewright Declaration, a "summation of the agreements made at the Housewright Symposium" (Hinckley 2000, 3).

1. All persons, regardless of age, cultural heritage, ability, venue, or financial circumstance deserve to participate fully in the best music experiences possible.

2. The integrity of music study must be preserved. Music educators must lead the development of meaningful music instruction and experience.
3. Time must be allotted for formal music study at all levels of instruction such that a comprehensive, sequential, and standards-based program of music instruction is made available.
4. All music has a place in the curriculum. Not only does the Western art tradition need to be preserved and disseminated, music educators also need to be aware of other music that people experience and be able to integrate it into classroom music instruction.
5. Music educators need to be proficient and knowledgeable concerning technological changes and advancements and be prepared to use all appropriate tools in advancing music study while recognizing the importance of people coming together to make and share music.
6. Music educators should involve the music industry, other agencies, individuals, and music institutions in improving the quality and quantity of music instruction. This should start within each local community by defining the appropriate role of these resources in teaching and learning.
7. The currently defined role of the music educator will expand as settings for music instruction proliferate. Professional music educators must provide a leadership role in coordinating music activities beyond the school setting to ensure formal and informal curricular integration.
8. Recruiting prospective music teachers is a responsibility of many, including music educators. Potential teachers need to be drawn from diverse backgrounds, identified early, led to develop both teaching and musical abilities, and sustained through ongoing professional development. Also, alternative licensing should be explored in order to expand the number and variety of teachers available to those seeking music instruction.
9. Continuing research addressing all aspects of music activity needs to be supported including intellectual, emotional, and physical responses to music. Ancillary social results of music study also need exploration as well as specific studies to increase meaningful music listening.
10. Music making is an essential way in which learners come to know and understand music and music traditions. Music making should be broadly interpreted to be performing, composing, improvising, listening, and interpreting music notation.

11. Music educators must join with others in providing opportunities for meaningful music instruction for all people beginning at the earliest possible age and continuing throughout life.

12. Music educators must identify the barriers that impede the full actualization of any of the above and work to overcome them. (219–20)

The Housewright Declaration served a dual purpose. It affirmed the recommendations of the Tanglewood Symposium and it brought to light new issues and challenges to be faced in the next two decades—shortages of music teachers, inadequate time for music instruction, community music education, and technological progress all demand visionary leadership.

THE NATIONAL ANTHEM PROJECT

MENC sponsored the National Anthem Project early in the twenty-first century. The project was intended "to restore America's voice through music education." The project was conceived in 2004, when a Harris poll found that few Americans knew the national anthem's history and only one of three knew its words. MENC began its campaign to teach the words and history with a traveling educational program that appeared in all fifty states, where a variety of musical events promoted familiarity with the national anthem.[1] First Lady Laura Bush was Honorary Chairperson, the Oak Ridge Boys the Official Musical Ambassadors, and the Jeep brand was the national sponsor. Other sponsors were the International Music Products Association, the History Channel, Bank of America, Gibson Musical Instruments, ASCAP, and Conn-Selmer, Inc. Supporters included Girl Scouts USA, the Walt Disney Company, the National Football League (NFL), the National Basketball Association (NBA), and the American Legion. The project had Congressional support. Representative Dennis Moore (D., Kansas) led the "House Blue Dog Coalition," a group of thirty-five moderate to conservative Democrats in the 109th Congress, in

---

1. Ironically, in 1930, when Congress was debating whether to adopt "The Star Spangled Banner" as the official national anthem, MENC (then the Music Supervisors National Conference) adopted a resolution against the bill. The *New York Times* reported that MSNC asserted that "the song was the outgrowth of a single historical event and was too difficult a musical composition to be rendered properly by school children, informal gatherings and public meetings where the singing of the national anthem was appropriate." MSNC preferred that "America the Beautiful" be adopted instead. Nevertheless, "The Star Spangled Banner" was approved by Congress in 1931 as the official national anthem of the United States.

supporting a $2.9 million appropriation request for the National Anthem Project. The project began in 2005 and continued through 2007.

THE NO CHILD LEFT BEHIND ACT

The principal legislation of the new century to affect music education was the reauthorization of the Elementary and Secondary Education Act, also known as the No Child Left Behind Act (NCLB), signed in January 2002. President George W. Bush called the act "a cornerstone of my administration." It was intended to level the field for all children, especially the underprivileged who were served by Title I.

NCLB required states to create and implement accountability standards and to determine success by testing students in curricular areas identified as core subjects. Title IX of the Act designated English, reading or language arts, mathematics, science, foreign languages, civics and government, economics, arts, history, and geography as the core academic subjects, but it did not identify the individual subjects that constituted the arts. One of the key components of NCLB was testing, which the law required only in reading, mathematics, and science. Congress left it to the states to decide which other subjects were to be tested.

NCLB created difficulties for music and other subjects for which testing was not required. High stakes testing in reading, mathematics, and science forced administrators and teachers to place more emphasis on preparing students in those areas, usually by increasing classroom time for them. That time was taken from other subjects, often music. The Center for Education Policy found that instructional time for school music and art had been reduced by 22 percent in 2006.

By 2006, every state except one[2] had established content standards in the arts. Forty-four states specifically require instruction in the arts (Education Commission of the States 2005). As more attention was given to testing reading and mathematics, teachers of other subjects were often required to relate their subjects to them. This was a new direction for music teachers. It affected what they taught and how they taught. Many music teachers had to find ways to correlate their subject matter content with the teaching of reading or mathematics.

The emphasis on testing created a new dynamic for American schools. Tests did not actually measure children's knowledge, but only whether

---

2. Local school districts in Iowa develop their own standards, and so there are no state standards.

schools successfully prepared students for the tests. Social commentator Andy Rooney said in his *60 Minutes* television segment on April 9, 2006:

> The new federal "No Child Left Behind" law, has changed a lot of things in school. . . . Reading and math are the only subjects tested by national exams, so schools are desperate to have their students do well in those subjects. . . . Something's wrong here. Any time teaching is done just to help kids pass an exam, it's wrong. The purpose of teaching is to provide an education, not to help kids pass a test. . . . Subjects like science, art, history, and music are being taught very little in a lot of schools. We're going to raise a generation of cultural idiots—people who don't know Beethoven from Mozart, Cezanne from Van Gogh, or Albert Einstein from Charles Darwin.

A positive aspect of NCLB for music education is that the arts were identified as core subjects. This is significant because national education programs like teacher training, school reform, and technology are eligible to receive federal funds. NCLB was the first instance of federal recognition of the arts as core subjects and their first inclusion in the Elementary and Secondary Education Act since it was originally passed by Congress in 1965.

THE MENC CENTENNIAL

In 2007, MENC celebrated the centennial of its founding in 1907 in Keokuk, Iowa. It also sponsored a Centennial Congress in Orlando, Florida, that featured speakers from the music education profession and from other national education organizations. The Congress culminated with the *Centennial Declaration*, written by Paul Lehman, Bennett Reimer, Janet Barrett, and Michael Mark:

> We are in agreement that the basic ideals long expressed by the music education profession and other education professionals are still current: It is the right of every child to receive a balanced, comprehensive, sequential music education taught by qualified music teachers.
>
> A healthy society requires musically fulfilled people. The primary purpose of education is not to create a workforce: it is to improve the quality of life for individuals and for society. Although music education has been valued throughout history for its unique contributions, it is not yet universal in American schools. Serious problems persist, including inequality of access, uneven quality of programs, and insufficient valuing of music as a part of the curriculum. As a result, music is often pushed to the periphery of the school experience. In this centennial year of 2007,

we reaffirm our longstanding ideals in a challenging context that calls for directed action in curriculum, assessment, research, teacher education, advocacy, and building alliances.

Needs Regarding Curriculum

Our curriculum must reflect more than our own desires; it must reflect the needs and desires of the students we serve. We seek contexts and modes of instruction that will provide students with more inclusive experiences of the styles and genres of music and the many musical roles that are practiced in our society and that are represented in the national content standards. We need to develop programs that are flexible and of greater variety than those currently in use in most schools. This will require efforts including identifying and promulgating effective models, rethinking teacher education, expanding inservice development opportunities, and developing new assessment techniques. These initiatives necessitate an expansion of our research interests and a greater application of research results in teacher education programs and in classrooms. We need to develop deeper insight into the role of music in general education, focusing on what is distinctive about music and its complementary relationship to other subjects. We need electives as broad and diverse as the interests and enthusiasms of our students.

Needs Regarding Assessment

We need assessment techniques and strategies that are suited to the domain of music in all its complexity and diversity. We need to focus our energies on the development of multiple assessment strategies that reflect the dimensions of students' musical growth and draw upon a broad range of instructional methodologies and techniques. We need assessment criteria that go beyond attendance, effort, and attitude. We need formative assessments of students' learning—including portfolios and other techniques, and we need program evaluations based on the Opportunity to Learn Standards.

Needs Regarding Advocacy

We need to arrive at ways to transmit a uniform message to decision makers and to the public. We need strong alliances with those who share or understand the value of music study and are willing to join with us in advocating for strong, vibrant music programs. We need to make advocacy efforts that clarify and celebrate the enhanced opportunities to learn that we are striving to make available.

Toward the Future

We will build on our first hundred years of success with a second century of leadership and service. Our musical culture, our students, and our society deserve no less.

TOPICS FOR THOUGHT AND DISCUSSION

1. Compare the reports of the Tanglewood Symposium, the Housewright Symposium, and the Centennial Congress. What influence have they had on the music education profession?
2. In what ways have the National Anthem Project helped MENC?
3. Discuss the effect of the No Child Left Behind Law on music education. Has it helped music education? Has it hurt it?

REFERENCES

Center on Education Policy (http://www.cep-dc.org). 2008.

Education Commission of the States. 2005. *State Notes: Arts in Education State Policies Regarding Arts in Education*. Denver: Education Commission of the States.

Hinckley, June. 2000. *Vision 2020. The Housewright Symposium on the Future of Music Education*, ed. Clifford Madsen. Reston, VA: Music Educators National Conference.

The MENC Centennial Declaration (http://menc.org/about/view/centennial-declaration). 2007.

CPSIA information can be obtained at www.ICGtesting.com
Printed in the USA
BVOW08s1223141115

426971BV00001B/2/P